# MATTER OF SPIRIT

# MATTER OF SPIRIT

*Elizabeth Barberi*

SPIRITUAL UNDERSTANDING NETWORK, LLC

MATTER OF SPIRIT


Spiritual Understanding Network, LLC
P.O. Box 48, Salisbury, CT 06068-0048

Further information available at:
**www.matterofspirit.com**

Cover photograph © K. V. Barberi
This edition is printed in the U.S.A.
using acid-free paper and soy ink.

FIRST EDITION May 2004

ISBN 0-9752531-0-7
Library of Congress Control Number: 2004091345

To Reverend Alvord Beardslee who
urged me to write

To my husband who provided me a
quiet, happy home in which to write

And to all who supported
me with love and prayer

Thank you

# TABLE OF CONTENTS

# Chapter One: **VISION**

I didn't know what I was coming down with. It wasn't the flu. I didn't feel sick. Whatever it was, I didn't have time for it. Final exams were only a week away. Using the force of my will I put it off. But it was still there, pressing in on me the next day. I pushed it away from me again. On the following day I could tell that I was coming down with it. There was nothing I could do to stop it. Worried about how little time I had, I glanced at my clock. It was two-thirty in the afternoon. It was coming on fast and it felt like it was going to be big. I needed to lie down quickly.

I flopped onto my bed face down. I felt weak, but not sick. Although my eyes were closed I was looking at things. It was as if I had stepped into a film or a dream that had no story; I was exploring a place I had never been. I would not have been so surprised by this experience if I had been asleep at the time. But I was awake. Just to be sure, I lifted my head and opened my eyes. Aha! There was my bedspread. And, look, there were the tiny holes I had made in it by plucking out some of the tufts when I was younger! I closed my eyes again, but the pictures resumed. Even though I was certain I was awake I decided to run one more test. I opened my eyes again and pinched my wrist to see if I could feel it. It hurt and I felt silly for having done it. I closed my eyes again to see what was going on inside my head.

I couldn't see clearly. I had the impression of being in a huge place that was grand and elegant. Everything was velvety black softness, spangled with gold. I felt a booming voice-like consciousness inside my head, a sudden knowing, "This is the Presence of God!" Awesome! I had never experienced anything like this.

Before I could open my eyes, the scene shifted. I was aware of myself being separate and apart from God. I was aware that my own self, my ego, was the center of my life. It was O.K. That's how it had been my whole life. But now I felt a tremendous longing for God. I ached to have God at the center of my being. I wanted to move from being self-centered to being God-centered. I tried to make that move. It was as if I could walk away from self-centeredness. But after a few steps I was drawn back to it. I became aware of two magnetic poles. One was egocentric and the other was God-centric. I wanted desperately to get to the God-centered pole. These two poles appeared to be about thirty feet apart. I set out for the God-centered pole, determined not to be pulled back. When I had gone about six feet, an invisible force dragged me back to where I had started. I made repeated attempts, each time digging my feet in more firmly than before. And each time I would lose my footing and slide back. I was desperate.

Even though I was caught up with this experience, I was still aware that I was lying on my bed. I was breathing heavily and my heart was pounding from the efforts I was making in the vision. My bedspread was getting wet with tears of frustration.

Never in my life had I wanted anything as much as I wanted to be at that God-centered pole. I struggled in every way that I could. In the vision I even clutched the ground, dragging myself forward on my belly until my energy was entirely gone. My clinging fingers made furrows in the ground as the unseen force dragged me back. I realized that I was unable to break out of the force field that held me at the self-centered pole. As soon as I had this thought, I saw Jesus standing beside me, wearing a long white robe. I almost laughed to see him there. I had recently come to the conclusion that we each make our own connection to God, and that it is unnecessary to have Jesus make that connection for us. Jesus put his arm around my shoulders and, with a touch as light as a feather, slid me effortlessly to the God-centric pole. With that the vision ended.

I got up from the bed deciding to rethink my opinions of Jesus. I took several steps toward the door, but then my knees began wobbling and came out from under me. I sat down hard on the floor. I was mistaken in thinking that the experience was over.

The pictures had ended, but now I heard voices. They were voices of people I knew well, and they were using words they had told me in the past month. First there was a sentence from my friend Nancy. It was followed by a sentence and a half my boyfriend had said on our last date. His half-sentence was completed by a half-sentence from a note Nancy had written to me. Next came the minister's voice with several sentences from a sermon two weeks earlier. And so it went for four or five minutes. It was wonderful. Woven together in this way, it explained the meaning of life. This was exciting…stunning! And then it was gone. Completely gone. In an instant, every single word was erased from my memory. It was so odd, as if someone had deleted it. I knew that I had heard all of the words before, in my waking life, and yet I couldn't recall a single one. Now I knew that life had meaning, even though I couldn't remember what it was. As I sat there on the floor, I felt like someone with a 5000-piece jigsaw puzzle. I knew I had all the pieces. It was up to me to figure out how to put them together.

I got to my feet, wondering how much time had been taken by this experience. I looked at the clock. Twenty minutes had passed since I had fallen onto my bed. Then I felt an inner urge to "put my house in order". I wasn't sure what that meant, but I immediately went to my parents to mend my relationship with them.

Afterward, I was stunned by the whole experience. Even though it seemed more deeply real than anything I had done before, it didn't fit into my thinking: my world-view or my theology. I didn't think Jesus was necessary or that visions were possible. I had been taught to think about God, not to experience God's presence and interaction. Having this vision set a course for my future: I wanted to understand what was going on.

*

I have spent years fitting together the pieces of the jigsaw puzzle. Some of the things I have learned, from books and from other people, ring true in my heart. As I shape my beliefs and understandings, I also have to make room for the spiritual experiences I have had. For some people, religion is an experience. For others it is a concept that guides their lives. My religious journey has taken me along both of these roads. It has been a wonderful trip that has brought me a lot of happiness.

I am writing this book hoping it may help someone else to find some of the happiness I have enjoyed. I believe that this is a path toward wholeness and that we become whole when our lives are fully interpenetrated by the Spirit of God. This, I feel, is the basic goal of many spiritual paths, and scriptures of various religions provide maps for how to get there. In this book I draw a new map. The destination is still the same, and this map uses many of the same roads. When we start on a long trip, it is helpful to have a current map. Old roads may have been renamed or replaced. There may be new expressways and junctions. If the only available map is old, it is necessary to stop frequently to get directions.

The spiritual journey involves every aspect of life.

There are new understandings about the body and the mind to add to the map. People are increasingly aware of their individuality and personal preferences. There is the realization that the motivations of deeds make a difference. Emotional freedom can be increased by opening up the subconscious mind. Success in business and sports can be improved by harnessing the power of imagination. As our sense of self expands, our relationship with God needs to expand along with it. We need to harmonize our entire self with God.

On this new map, the destination of the spiritual journey is still the same. Among the new roads are the use of imagination, dreams and intuition. Those paths have always been there and were taken occasionally by prophets. But in our times these routes have become expressways carrying a lot of traffic. I also include in this map some roads that have never changed, like doing acts of kindness. I try to mark these roads clearly so that people don't miss them. I describe a little of the scenery along the way and warn people about potholes I have seen. I don't describe all the possible routes in the spiritual journey. I tell about the one I have taken. I weave together thoughts and experiences to try to explain where I have been traveling. Some of the things I point out may interest you and others may not. I hope you may find something in this account that is helpful to you.

# Chapter Two: **INTERACTIVE GOD**

When I look at nature, it stirs something deep in the center of my being. It is as if I wake up to an awareness that the world and I are part of a great Oneness. The beauty of plants and flowers, little animals and birds, fills my heart with happiness. My heart overfills when I see the glory of a sunset or when I watch in silence as the dark of night gives way to gray and then bursts into the colors of day. I feel a peace come into me when I walk barefoot in morning grass still wet with dew, or listen to soft wind in the trees, or sit beside flowing water. At these times I know deep within me that the world has a creator, and I feel certain that the creator and all of the natural world are good.

I remember a special day when I was eighteen. It was the first day of my summer vacation from school. There was a warm breeze, fragrant with flowers and fresh cut grass. Birds chirped and a few insects buzzed through the air. "A perfect day," I thought, as I sat on the grass digging in the soft soil with my hand. The warm earth felt so good that I let my hand lie there covered in the warmth of the earth. It was a wonderful feeling, like having my hand held in the gentle embrace of a large and loving hand. My heart began to expand with happiness. Suddenly everything was clearer than before. It all looked more real than normal. In my eyes, everything was sparkling fresh and glowing. I felt as if I was one with all creation. My mind shouted, "I want to be one with God!" and I felt certain that I would do everything I could to accomplish it. I really wasn't sure what all this meant. The words had bubbled up out of the center of my being. I had seen the God-ness in creation and my heart responded. At that moment God felt as close to me as my own breath.

There have been other times when, looking at the awesome hugeness of God's creation, I almost forgot to breathe. These are times when I have looked out at the ocean, or at great expanses of land. I love to go up into high places where I can look out into the distance. It stirs something in me. I know then in the deepest, truest part of me that God is Infinite. Everything is included in this awesome oneness. There is no place or thing outside God. If there were, then God would have limits. And I know in my gut that God is unlimited. At night when I look at the stars that go on and on without stopping, I feel tiny. I am blown away by the greatness of God.

Since God is infinite, everything that exists must be

made out of God-stuff. (Surely God did not go to a store to get materials to make planets.) There is no thing and no place that is outside God. I believe that before the beginning of the universe there weren't things. There was only that which we call God or Spirit. Some of this Spirit morphed into solid form, becoming the atoms that make up everything in the physical world. The very substance of the universe is God. We might think of the process of creation as a sort of cosmic pasta-maker. Oneness passes through this form-giver and becomes individuated. The individual pieces of pasta are still made of the original stuff, but the appearance has changed. We, like everything else in the universe, are made of Oneness, though each of us is formed as a unique individual. To really understand ourselves we need to remember both of these aspects of our nature: oneness and individuality.

Physically and visibly we are individuals. But we are each one with all that is. We are made of God-stuff, and so is everything else. Since everything that exists has God as its source, we can be reminded intuitively of God by anything we meet. We can see God's presence in the land and all that lives on it. When we begin to see God in creation we begin to experience God for ourselves. This moves us from just having an idea of God, the Infinite, to experiencing that God *is* in everything and everything is in God.

*

God is constantly interacting with people. I have felt love from God, and many other people have too. This love from God has felt to me like a loving relationship between a parent and a child. Some people experience it more like the relationship between lovers. I do not understand how this relationship happens, but I can't deny it because I have experienced it myself.

Even though I have interacted with God, it is hard for me to be in touch with the friendliness of God while thinking about the infinity of God. When I think of the awesome hugeness of God it amazes me that interaction, communication, and relationship can exist between an individual and All That Is. I hear that the cells in my body have ways to exchange information and work for the good of the whole. But when we speak of an individual in relationship with a whole that is infinite, the idea is staggering. Like many people, I wonder, "Who am I, God, that you would notice me?" But God does notice. God cares about you and me as individuals. God is present to me every moment of life, and yet in some ways God is totally beyond my experience.

How can God be the awesome, unknowable infinite and at the same time be as close as breath and as kind as a loving person? These qualities seem contradictory, so we wonder how both could be true. Since God is infinite, God includes everything. So, with God, when one thing is true, something that seems to be opposite can also be true. This is complicated. Simple answers are easier. When people discuss God, these seemingly opposite qualities (paradoxes) may come up.

A person who understands just one end of a paradox sometimes argues with someone who is at the other end. Even though they are holding opposite positions, neither position is wrong. Expanding the concept of God to include both ends of a paradox leads to greater truth, but this truth may be too big to be understood. Sometimes we wish we could put God in a small enough package to be understandable, but anything small enough to be understood is not God.

*

Even though we can't comprehend God, we can feel God's activity if we are open to it. The first time I remember feeling this was when I was about eight years old. I lived in a safe neighborhood and was allowed to walk home by myself after dark. To get to my house I had to pass through a very dark area where large trees blocked the light from the streetlight. I would always feel a bit frightened as I hurried through this place. One night I got the idea of saying the prayer Jesus taught as I walked through the dark. When I did, my heart felt stronger and didn't tremble as it had before. This surprised me. I had never heard of using this prayer outside of a church service and I didn't expect it to have this effect. I felt protected.

A lot of people have felt protected by God. Thousands of years ago people were describing God as a protector, a shield, a strong wall, and a fort. Of course they didn't mean that God was some wood or metal shield. They used the word 'shield' symbolically. God's protection reminded them of the protection they could get from a shield. There have been many times when I have felt God's protection and care. I have driven many miles in my life. On two occasions my car skidded dangerously. As the car spun out of control, I called out, "God be with me!" Each time, my car came to an abrupt stop, in spite of great momentum which otherwise would have caused a crash. I have talked to people of various religions who have had similar experiences.

When I have been protected by God I have felt more as if I was being protected by a person than by an object. When I bump into the power of God, there seems to be a person-like presence connected to it. It's not that I see or hear anybody. But there are vibes like those that come from people. I don't know why or how that is the case, but I suppose it is one of the reasons that God has been described as a father. Sometimes when I ask for God's protection it awakens in me a sense of security. It is the same feeling of security that came when I was a little child being lovingly held by one of my parents.

God can be a source of strength. A man I knew told me about an experience he had. He was caught in a terrible snowstorm as he walked home. He had to cross a bridge where the wind was fierce. The wind was so strong that he was unable to go forward and so cold he was sure he would die. He prayed for strength, promising to be faithful to God in his Islamic faith. At that moment he found in himself the strength to get across the bridge and to the safety of his home. He knew that the strength had come from God, and he found God's power awesome. He was equally amazed that God had entered into his own personal life.

*

God seems to delight in helping us when we realize that our own power is not enough for the situation we are in. We need to admit that we can't handle it on our own. And we need to ask God for help. (Some people want so much to be in control that they would rather die than ask for help.) God is the source of life and healing. Sickness has brought many people to the point where they became open to the power of God.

A friend invited me to go with her to hear a spiritual healer talk about healing through prayer. The healer, Olga Worrell,[1] said that a person is more likely to receive healing if he holds a certain attitude. In addition to wanting to be healed, it is important to be willing to let go of the illness. Sometimes being sick has fringe benefits to enjoy, such as getting sympathy from others or having less work to do. It is useful to make the clear decision to be willing to give up the sickness and all that goes with it. Paradoxically, it is useful, at the same time, to be willing to accept the illness, if continuing to have it will bring additional learning and spiritual growth.

Later in the day there was a time when people in the audience could go to the front of the room for healing. I sat in the front row to see what would happen. This

---

1 (Notes begin on page 165.)

event was being held in a church. Instead of doing the healing herself, Worrell had invited three local pastors to come to prayerfully lay their hands on the heads of people who wanted to be healed. These men had never done this sort of thing before. There was an empty chair in front of each pastor. Each person who wanted healing had a turn to sit in a chair to be touched by one of the pastors. The pastor prayed that God's healing energy would flow through his hands to this person. Meanwhile, Olga Worrell was also praying for everyone. She had said not to be shy about asking for healing. The problem didn't need to be a big one. It only needed to be something you were willing to let go of.

I decided to see if I could be cured of a very minor infection I had had for a couple of years. It didn't bother me. I only knew about it because doctors had occasionally mentioned it. The pastor who was available when my turn came looked insecure. He placed one hand on my head and the other on my back. In my mind I reviewed my willingness to be without this condition. I could hear the pastor mumbling a prayer too softly for me to understand. Then I remembered to add to my own prayer that if I could learn from this problem I would willingly accept the condition. The moment I got to the part about accepting it, the pastor jerked his hands and blurted out with astonishment, "You're being healed! Go sit in your seat!" Feeling healing energy, which can sometimes tingle like a small electrical current, probably startled him. I didn't feel it myself, but I returned to my seat. About ten minutes later I had a peculiar sensation as if a bubble was wandering around just beneath my skin in the area of the infection. It made me think that something had actually happened. Two weeks later the infection was gone. I was impressed.

Another opportunity to see God's healing power came because a car hit me and broke my arm. The hospital x-rays of my forearm showed that the broken ends of the ulna were not quite in the right position. The doctor refused to reset the bone because its ends were in "seventy percent apposition". That meant that only part of the bone surfaces matched up. He said that more bone material would build up around the break and my bone would be strong enough. The doctor had me come to his office each week for two new x-rays and a new cast.

After the second of these office visits a friend asked if I wanted any prayers for my arm. I told him there was no pain but I wished the doctor had reset the bone. I didn't need the pieces of bone to be 100% in contact, but 70% didn't seem good enough. I asked him if prayer could change the position of the bone. He didn't know, but thought it was worth a try. Five days later, during a nap, I reached suddenly for something I saw in my dream. I woke up with pain in my arm.

When I had my weekly x-rays two days later, the doctor was shocked. My arm had reset itself inside the cast! He had three sets of x-rays showing the bones with 70% contact. Now the contact was 90%. I was delighted and I thanked God.

*

Receiving healing, strength and protection are among the ways people have experienced God's action in their lives. These gifts only come if they are asked for. It isn't absolutely necessary to believe in God, though it helps. There needs to be at least the open-minded view that God might exist and have the ability to heal. A person's first prayer might be, "God, if there is a God, if you are capable of healing this problem, and if you are willing to heal me, I would like to be healed." My arm was probably reset to 90% because I had been holding the attitude, "I don't need 100%". Now I realize that God could have done 100%, but my attitude blocked it. True open-mindedness places no blocks.

Another way people experience God is as a source of supply. I once met a young woman who traveled around the country "living on faith". She constantly prayed for God to provide her with everything she needed. She had no home or money, but found a safe place to sleep every night. She believed God directed her to these places because of her prayers. She told of one time she and a few other people were in an abandoned house but had no food. After she prayed for food, a man came to the house with a bag of groceries, which he gave to them. He said that he had a feeling that he was supposed to bring food there though he didn't know why.

I know a lot more examples of God providing what is needed. The first few times it happens in your own life there is a temptation to say that the supply had nothing to do with the prayer for it. They occurred at the same time only by coincidence. But many people who continue experimenting with prayer become convinced that these 'coincidences' come far too frequently to be by coincidence.

*

After having experiences like these it is no surprise that people have described God as Protector, Healer, Provider and Strength. These are not definitions of God, because God is so much more. Each is just one of an uncountable number of aspects of God. The Bible gives many different examples so that we do not fall into thinking that one way to look at God is the whole story. God is described as being like a rock, a fort or a powerful river. God is like a mother bird that protects her chicks under her wings. God is Light. God is Love. Sometimes God is described much like a person. God is like a good parent; like a loving partner in marriage. God is like a person who feeds and protects defenseless animals. God cares about every little bird that falls from the sky. These terms are used because God has so often been experienced as a personality, as one who loves, and as part of an intimate relationship. Yet an experience of God is not quite like an experience with another human. It goes beyond normal experiences. It is hard to find words that would accurately describe the experience to someone else.

We need to struggle to find words that express what we have experienced of God. God is the greatest source of power. How can I describe this? The power-words of ancient times no longer express power. I might use terms like "life force" or "electric energy" or "empowerment." But even these words are not really accurate. I have to hunt around for words from the physical world to describe things that are not physical. The match is not exact. The words will always fall short of accuracy. God never will be adequately described in words. But that's O.K. We worship the Holy One behind the words, represented by the words. The words are words. We worship the One to whom they point.

*

Since our minds cannot take in the immensity of God, it is fortunate that God is willing to meet us in these many particular ways. The Bible has about 200 metaphors for God. Similarly, Islamic Scripture lists 99 "Most Beautiful Names of God". Any of God's attributes can become a portal to deep and satisfying connection to God. God has been experienced in a multitude of ways including the total absence of anything. Being the ultimate Oneness, God can be experienced as fullness or emptiness, everything or nothing, light or darkness. God's existence can be revealed through anything we are capable of experiencing.

Any one of God's attributes can connect a person to God. However there is no thing or relationship that can fully reflect God. None of us can see everything. We each have our own perspective. We see things from where we are standing. When I stand outside a building and look at it, I am not seeing what the building looks like from the inside. When I look at the front of the building I can't see the back of it.

Let's consider something even bigger than a building: the ocean. There are many ways to see the ocean. People on the shore are filled with awe and peace by watching the ocean from a distance. A sailor has a vivid experience of the ocean without ever going under the surface of the water. The ocean floor can be looked at from so many locations and directions that no one person could ever see all of it, even though it is of limited size. To learn about the ocean, oceanographers share with each other what they have seen.

God is much bigger than the ocean. Many people through the centuries have had experiences with God. Since God is infinite it would be strange if there were only a small number of ways for God to be experienced. Each person may see a different aspect, customized to the individual's personality and situation. The fact that there is more than one view of God should be reassuring to us, since God is infinite. It would make sense for people to share their experiences of God with each other, instead of wondering who has the best view. Since God is unlimited, we could never know all there is to know about God. We each have an individual viewpoint. Yet wherever we stand, we can have an experience of God. God meets us where we are. I will share my experiences of God with you, and I hope you will find opportunities to share your own insights and experiences with others. Many of the experiences I have had of God's presence and power have come when I was praying for God to send healing energy through me to other people.

*

I joined a meditation group when I was twenty-seven. Each week we discussed spiritual issues raised in a book called *A Search for God*,[2] each of us giving our own views and experiences on the topic. Our ideas varied a lot and our appreciation of the viewpoints of one another grew as months rolled by. After talking about God for an hour we would spend twenty minutes in silence, focusing on a concept like, "Lord, let me be a channel of your blessings to others." At the end of the silence, we each had a turn to pray for God's healing for ourselves, or for people who had asked us for prayers. When the prayer time ended there were announcements of upcoming events.

I enjoyed the meetings enough to attend two or three times a month. After a year and a half one of these meetings ended differently for me. During the prayer time I felt an odd sensation in my fingers. It was the 'warm tingly glow' that I had sometimes felt when helping another person, but this time it was only in my fingers. The tingly feeling was moving out through the tips of my fingers, as if my fingers were stuck in the end of a vacuum cleaner. The sensation continued while people began to chat. It was such an unusual experience for me that I mentioned it to the group. I was told, "Oh, that's healing energy. You just sit there and continue to pray while we go on with the discussion."

In the months that followed I continued to feel things going on in my hands when I prayed. I stopped having the sensations in my fingers, but a small tingly hot spot would come in the center of my palms. It gradually became larger over a period of weeks, until it was about the size of a quarter. Over the years since then, I usually feel something in my hands when I pray, but not always. I am glad that I am able to feel the gentle sensations that come during these special moments. When I do feel healing energy, it reminds me of a very low voltage electrical current. Frequently when I pray I feel this charge throughout my entire body. The sensation most similar to this is orgasm. (I am speaking from a woman's point of view.) In sexual orgasm the electrical charge is all bunched up in one area of the body and is very strong. In healing prayer, the energy is gentler, and it can be diffused throughout the whole body.

The helpfulness of the prayers seems to remain the same whether I feel anything or not. Many people do not feel the energy as it flows through them, but healing energy moves through them whether they feel it or not. I think feeling the energy is a matter of sensitivity. I think some people are more sensitive than others to healing energy. Some people are more aware of dust than others because they are hypersensitive to it. It makes them sneeze even though they do not actually breathe more of it than other people do. In the same way, one person may feel more energy than another because of being more aware of energy. It does not necessarily mean that there is more healing energy flowing through that person than through someone who does not feel it. I have seen that I do not need to feel special sensations for my prayers to be effective.

I had a friend, ill from copper toxicity, who requested

weekly healing prayer. While I prayed for her I would place my hand on or above her head. One evening while I prayed for her I felt absolutely no energy flowing through my hands. It surprised me because I had thought both of us were strongly tuned into God that evening. But I thought it would be silly to keep up the appearance of doing healing prayer if, in fact, nothing was happening. While I was thinking these thoughts, my eyes opened, and I could see my hand about six inches above my friend's head. Then I was startled to see that there was so much electrical energy between my hand and her head, that some of her hair was standing straight up so that the tips of the hairs were touching my hand. I realized that something was happening even though I felt nothing. I closed my eyes again and continued to pray. After the prayer time my friend said that the energy had felt especially strong that night.

*

I feel very connected to God when I do healing prayer. Being a channel of God's energy is the approach I have used most to gain a sense of oneness with God. I learned about this type of prayer at the meditation group. I was told to ask in prayer that God's healing energy would flow through me, directed by my thoughts to those who had asked for prayer. I was surprised by the idea that God's healing energy could flow through me. The person explaining healing prayer said, "In the Bible Jesus makes some promises. It is possible that he knew what he was talking about. Find out what those promises are. Experiment with them. Try them and see if they work." One of the things Jesus claimed was that people who followed his path would be able to do the things he did, and even more. Jesus was a powerful healer, so experimenting with healing seemed to be a good place to start.

In most cases, I have experienced God's activity because I was willing to experiment with it. I was willing to let God take action in some area of my life. I didn't have to already *believe* in God's capability; I only needed to be open-minded about the *possibility* of God acting in my life. I had to be willing to have an experience. God respects our wills. If we choose not to experience God, we don't have to. As for me, I have been doing a lot of experimenting, and I'm very happy with the results.

These are not random experiences. I have been having experiences like these for thirty years, and they only happen when I am focused on something that reminds me of God. Is it any wonder that I consider God to be interactive? The experiences I have described are not unusual for people who develop relationship with God through prayer and meditation.[3]

I have had other experiences that are unique to the personal relationship between God and me. There have been some visions, some insights and some spiritual gifts. These are spiritual gifts, not acquisitions. They are not something that a person ever "deserves" or earns. Yet I find that each seems to come only after I have put what I have already received into use, doing what I understand to be God's work. Why would we be given gifts if we had a history of not using them? Why would we get guidance if we never follow it? Why would we get insight into ourselves if we were unwilling to change? The interaction with God is a relationship. It is so highly interactive that it is influenced by each thing I do, say or think toward others, and even toward myself. One person who has cultivated a relationship with God describes it as, "...the wordless song...the musicless dance. Who is leading whom?"[4]

I have not had every type of "commonly occurring" spiritual experience. I have never suddenly fallen unconscious when receiving healing prayer. But then, I have never been in direct contact with someone whose healing touch had that reputation. So I don't know if it would happen to me. I have spoken to a few people who have had that experience. One said that, for about 12 hours afterward, her body odor smelled like perfume even though she bathed and changed her clothes. She never had any other experience like it in her life. She was so startled that she didn't want to tell anyone about it for years. Her husband found out about it because he could see a change in her face and because he couldn't figure out where the smell of roses was coming from.

I can sympathize with her embarrassment about discussing this experience with her friends. I remember two occasions when I felt overcome with joy about God's goodness. I felt as if I should speak out loud in some way to express my gratitude. It was contrary to my religious upbringing to pray aloud. I didn't know what to say and just allowed God to provide the words. But what came out was a sort of baby-talk babble. I felt embarrassed and stopped it even though there was no one who could hear. I expect that this is what is called "speaking in tongues". I have never heard anyone else do it. I hear that there are some churches where it happens often. I have heard people question whether all the "speaking in tongues" occurrences are true spiritual experiences. They wonder if a person could get into it by a sort of placebo effect of desire and expectation. Perhaps. Negative feelings like fear and panic seem to be able to transfer among people, so it would be reasonable that joyful feelings could also spread in a group setting. But I don't think it is wise to judge other people's spiritual experiences. If my judgment were incorrect I might be denying the activity of God's Spirit, which I'd rather not do.

Some people have very intense experiences of God's presence and power. It is easy for them to assume that the type of experience they had is the best, and perhaps the only, way to come to know God. But that would suggest that God is limited. I do not think that anyone has experienced all the types of spiritual gifts God has to offer. I believe there is far more to God than anyone can handle. God is not limited, but we are. We do not need to experience everything that is possible to occur between God and humans. Being merciful, God meets each of us where we are. In our personal lives opened to God's love, truth and power, we can come to the experience, the certainty, that God IS.

# Chapter Three: **DANCE OF THE SOUL**

I believe God is infinite. Everything that exists owes its origin to God. God is the source of my body and the life force in it. As the creator of my body, God makes it possible for my body to convert food into energy; God is the source of plants that become the food for people and animals; God's life-force is in each seed; God is the source of the sun, air and water the plants must have. These God-given factors supply the energy I use in my daily activities. I may even receive additional energy from God when I ask for it in prayer. It is clear to me that God is the source of all of my energy.

The energy God gives me is pure, unformed energy. The energy takes form as I use it for thoughts, words and deeds. These expressions I make are shaped by my attitudes, emotions and desires. If I feel angry, the energy I use at that time is likely to manifest as an angry word or action. Like batter poured into a pan, God's life-giving energy will be shaped by the emotion that receives it. It is a shame to use energy that comes as a gift from God in ways that are contrary to the source from which it comes. I look at my daily life in a new way when I realize that my energy is really God's energy. When I feel as if I am working in partnership with God, I become more patient, cheerful and careful in many of my activities. I also notice that when I do kind things for other people I have more energy available than usual. It seems that the closer my activity comes to being in harmony with God, the longer my energy lasts. After I pray for someone who has asked for God's healing, I find I have more energy than when I started!

On the other hand, I have sometimes wasted a lot of energy in non-productive ways. There have been times I have used up an entire day's supply of energy by pouring it into worry. It's very tiring to worry. I can't get much else done if I use all my available energy in worry. Other energy-wasters are self-pity, jealousy, criticalness, and resentment. It was very helpful to me when I realized that all these expressions are powered by a single God-given energy. The energy I waste in worry could have been used for healing prayer. I have a choice about how I use my energy; I have a lot of possible ways to pattern God's energy in my life. I can make an effort to shape my actions with the best patterns I have in me.

Even if I have difficulty letting go of a troublesome attitude, I can stop putting time and energy into it. Some people I know have broken a troublesome habit by finding a better way to use the energy. A friend of mine could not control her feelings of jealousy. Every day she sent huge amounts of energy flowing through the emotional pattern of jealousy. She tried to suppress her jealousy, but she had put so much energy into it, she couldn't keep the jealousy down. She needed to find a new way to use up some of this energy. My friend also had a pattern of chronic lateness. As a way to use up energy, she pushed herself hard to be on time in all that she did. She poured vast amounts of energy into punctuality, completing tasks long before they were due. She soon realized that she felt less jealous. She literally didn't have as much energy to put into feeling jealous! Another friend realized that he became less likely to make critical remarks to his family when, at his business meetings, he began standing up for what he believed. It was still the same energy, but he was using it in a more constructive way.

*

Many of us find that we get stuck in some undesired pattern of behavior. We may not want to act that way but find it very hard to change our habit. Often these strong behavior patterns involve emotions that are related to our hormones. The glands usually involved are the thymus (love), the adrenals (protection), and of course the gonads (sex).

Each of these glands, combined with the related emotion/desire, has been called a *chakra* or spiritual center in the body. It is a place where God's energy makes strong connection with the physical body.[5] The Bible does not have a word equivalent to chakra. But the Bible does make it clear that our relationship to God is strongly affected by the way we use sexual or adrenal energy (fear, anger or courage), as well as by the question of who or what we love.

The activities of the gonads, adrenals and thymus have such strong effects on our bodies that we can feel the impact when they are deeply moved. Falling in love produces one of the most wonderful sensations we can feel. But we can also feel a "broken heart".

We can also feel fear. Whenever I am anxious I feel the muscles above my navel tighten. I get this sensation regardless of what causes my anxiety. It can result from hearing my home make creaking sounds or from seeing strangers walk toward me in a dangerous neighborhood.

Worry is a big energy waster. It is easy to slip into worrying, and I have done a lot of worrying over the years. I used to walk around for hours with my gut tense before I woke up to the fact that I was worried. Then I learned to be alert to the muscles of my torso. I realized that these muscles tighten up whenever I am worried about something. When I focus my attention on God's power and protection, my fears go away. I know that worrying is harmful to my health so I pray as soon as I realize I am worried. Now, when these muscles are tight (which alerts me that I am anxious), I say a quick prayer, "God be with me," to call God's presence into my mind.

After making a habit of praying each time my gut tightened, I discovered a big bonus. One night I had a nightmare. Because I was frightened, my gut muscles tightened. Even though I was asleep, my mind was aware of the tightened muscles. I began talking in my sleep saying, "God be with me!" which instantly ended the scary dream and woke me up. A few months later I had another nightmare. Again I began praying within the dream because of the tensed muscles. This time I remained asleep, but the dream instantly stopped being scary and had a good ending. After that I had no nightmares for many years.

*

Shortly after I learned that it is possible to redirect energy I found myself sexually attracted to a man other than my husband. The attraction was very strong. My head and heart did not want to be romantically involved with him, but my body was excited. Our activities caused us to meet once or twice a week. I was careful not to show how I felt, but I was tongue-tied when I spoke to him and my hands were sweaty. I could hardly sleep at night. After several exhausting weeks I was desperate. It felt as if a huge amount of energy was bunched up in one part of my body. Then I remembered that this was some of God's energy and that I could use it in other ways. I decided to try to move the big wad of energy out of there. I prayed as hard as I could that God would help me push this energy up out of my gonads. I wanted to raise it to the most spiritual part of me, so that this energy from God could be reshaped and sent out to others as healing prayer.

For about forty-five minutes I prayed, using the force of my will to visualize the mass of energy being pushed upward. Sometimes I felt the energy move upward a little; at other times it got stuck. Finally I felt that the energy had reached the center of my head. I dedicated the energy to God's use, which re-formed the energy. Then I prayed for God to send it out as healing energy. Immediately I felt the glowing sensation of healing prayer flowing out of me, and experienced a great sense of release. When I finished praying for others to be healed, I realized that I no longer felt any physical attraction to that man. I never again felt sexually attracted to him, even for a moment. I had been able to convert the energy from one use (sexual attraction) to another (healing prayer). Certainly I had prayed very hard, but even so, I was surprised by how simple it was to do.

*

I continue to have "opportunities" to redirect energy. Blasts of emotions that used to knock me off balance have now become spiritual opportunities. The stronger the energy flowing into an emotion, the greater the potential energy I can put into God's service. I have "raised" energy that festered in me in the forms of anxiety and fear. I give it to God to be used in appropriate ways. Once I felt outraged over feeling unfairly treated. With some effort I managed to raise up to the top of my head the intense feeling that had been centered in my gut. After I felt the energy releasing its hold on my adrenals I prayed that God would use the energy to do good. Afterward, I felt calmer inwardly and could deal with my situation in a way that was in harmony with my spiritual values.

When I "raise" energy, I visualize myself removing the energy from the pattern it is in and giving it to God (not just asking God to get it). I imagine it releasing its grip on my body and emotions. Many times I have given God energy that was causing turmoil in me. Each time I have immediately felt wonderful peacefulness. If you have difficulty understanding how to "move" energy you probably expect it to be harder than it is. Energy responds to visualizations, imaginations, and daydreams, and to requests stated in words. If we think about the energy and have a strong desire about where we want it to go, it usually will go there. Energy seems to be moved by thought. Our thoughts and strong desires do much to direct God's energy in us. They are like molds that shape our activities.

It is very important to understand the power of desire to shape lives. This is because we have desires that are shaping our lives, whether or not we are aware of it. Most people have an idea about what kind of life they would like to have. Some primarily desire to be happy; others may prefer to be famous, or well liked, or financially secure. If a person holds a strong desire to become wealthy it will probably affect his choice of career, clothing and friends, and possibly even his choice of spouse. A primary desire to be at peace or to be kind could easily result in a different set of choices. Because your desires lead your life, it is important that the desires you hold will lead where you want your life to go. Many people, late in their careers, regret that they had been so focused on money that they had spent little time on loving relationships. Jesus mentioned that a person's life could not be guided both by God and by the desire for money. Each person must decide which of these gets preference when it comes to making choices.

*

Probably the most important kind of choice you can make in your life is to consciously choose what you want to have guide your life. I call a pattern or desire that I choose to guide my life my *ideal*.[6] I hope the energy coming into my life will take this pattern. Ideals are inspirational, leading us to be better than we are, in ways such as "truthfulness", "kindness" or "forgiveness". An ideal can be used for a short time, like six months. Sometimes people use as their ideal a quality that is missing in their life, such as "peace" or "balance". They use that quality as the pattern for their own thoughts and actions. When I tried that myself it certainly had a big effect on my life. After choosing "balance" as my ideal I met the man who is now my husband. His personality and abilities balance mine in many ways and we have been blessed with a very happy marriage. A lot of people use as their ideal the kind of love that Jesus taught and lived.

One of my favorite ideals is "Dear God, use me as a channel of your blessing to others." I often bring this ideal to my mind when I pray. Doing this over a period of time, I find that I become more attentive to how I treat other people. That tends to improve my interactions, which in turn improves my life. So when I try to be a channel of blessings to other people, it ends up as a blessing in my own life as well.

I like to focus on my ideal for several minutes every day. This helps the ideal make a deep impression in my consciousness so that it will be more likely to shape my actions. The desires we let our hearts and minds dwell on most often are more likely to shape our actions.

Selecting an ideal to guide my life has been the single most important step of my inner journey. I have found that once I commit myself to an ideal, it has tremendous impact on my life. The impact goes beyond the fact that the ideal I choose influences the choices I make. Unexplainably, it seems to draw the quality of that ideal into my life. I found this happening as soon as I started experimenting with ideals.

One week, everyone in my meditation group decided to experiment with the ideal of "patience". We were a varied group, including a range of educational and economic backgrounds. We ranged in age from early twenties to mid-eighties. Some had just started a spiritual journey; others had walked it for years. But each of us wanted, in our own way, to begin to bring patience into our lives. The next week we discussed our experiences. The first person said, "This was a terrible week to have the ideal of patience! The kids were sick and my mother-in-law came for a visit. My patience was stretched to its limit." The next person said, "You think *your* patience was tested? Wait until I tell you what my boss did this week…" And so it went, around the group. Everyone had had to use patience far more than usual. It gave us a sense that God had been listening to our plans about bringing patience into our lives. It seemed that God had responded as if to say, "Do you want to know about patience? O.K…here, try this!" As you can see from this example, the spiritual path isn't always *easy*, but it can be interesting, surprising and sometimes even funny. I suggest that you not take patience for your ideal until you feel ready for it!

Choose as your ideal a quality that you truly desire to have in your life right now. We all have a lot to learn and we don't have to learn it all the same day. When your ideal has helped you to grow you will be ready for more. It is helpful for people who have an over-arching ideal to "be like Jesus" or "be One with God" to focus, one at a time, on various aspects of their ideal. These aspects include qualities such as tolerance, forgiveness, kindness, generosity, and helpfulness.

Jesus said to treat people the way we would like to be treated. I have seen the attitudes I hold toward other people come back to me. It is a gradual process, which may take years. The person who becomes generous toward me is a different person than the one with whom I was generous. And yet I find that I harvest in my own life "seeds" I have sown in the lives of other people. We learn by making choices about how to act, and then harvesting the consequences of those choices.

If we were quick learners we would soon learn to live the loving, non-judgmental life recommended by many great spiritual leaders. I wish I were a quick learner, but I'm not.

*

Even though I choose as my ideal to be a channel of God's blessings, I can forget that during a difficult day. My subconscious mind, however, doesn't forget. It keeps track of the ideal I chose and compares it with my actions during the day. At night my dreams may show me that my actions were less than a blessing to someone in my life that day. Since I would like to be a better channel of God's blessings, I appreciate this nighttime coaching. (I am only shown as much as I am ready and able to do.) As I make my way in my spiritual journey I sense that I have a wonderful and caring coach telling me how to improve. I have come to love my dreams.

Dreams will coach people who have chosen an ideal for their life. If we set a standard (an ideal) and try to live that way, God will let us know how we are doing. It is necessary, though, that we learn how to interpret our dreams.

Dreams are symbolic. They cannot usually be understood as if they were news reports. The vehicle in your dream may represent your body. The people in the dream may represent different sides of your personality. To interpret dreams we need to understand symbolism.[7] Our dreams are not presented in symbols just to make them hard to understand. They are coming from the intuitive level in our minds, which is in symbolic language. We spent a few years, as children, learning the language we hear each day. We also need to spend time learning the language our minds use at night. It is well worth the effort to learn how to understand dreams. Many issues raised in dreams are important to spiritual growth.

*

There is nothing peculiar about being in contact with God.[8] It is a basic human ability, although it requires paying attention to the intuitive side of the brain. Dreaming is an everyday altered state of consciousness we all have. It is a wonderful resource, and a pity to waste. Dreams are about the easiest way to get inner guidance, because the outer senses are sleeping. With practice many people learn to be attentive to intuitive guidance that comes to them during their waking hours. This is a human potential. I find it necessary to have some quietness in my life to get in touch with inner feelings. If my day is packed end-to-end with talk and activity my attention is always drawn outward. I can't become aware of what is going on inside me.

Inward feeling can provide useful information. For example, how do you feel when you hear about some activity that has been planned? Do you feel good about it or does the plan make you feel restless and tense? Many parents around the world have had intuitive feelings like these that have helped them protect their children. One day a friend of mine didn't feel comfortable sending her little boy to school, so she kept him at home. The school bus he normally rode had an accident that day, but her son was not hurt because she had kept him home. Intuition saved my own son, too. Once late at night I felt that I should go look at my baby as he slept. When I got close to the crib I could hear him breathing with great difficulty. He was so oxygen-deprived that I could not wake him up. I was able to save his life by blowing air into his mouth. The intuitive feeling that sent me to my baby was not my first useful inner feeling I had ever had. But it certainly convinced me to always keep open to my intuitive side.

Some people are also treated to waking visions. When I was a teenager, a classmate told me that she had seen an angel in her bedroom. It stood quietly in the corner of the room every night. Her parents were arguing a lot at that time and the angel's presence gave my friend the sense that she was being protected by God. At the time she told me about it, I assumed it was some kind of hallucination because my concept of "reality" was quite physical. I changed my mind a year later when I had the visionary experience that I described at the beginning of this book. That experience had no angel in it, but it opened my mind. Reports of angels are found in many cultures and throughout the centuries. I have read the experiences of people who, after being dead briefly, were brought back to life by medical technology. Many of these people reported seeing "a being of light" or "an angel" or "Christ" during the time they were clinically dead. Surely angels are not physical, and yet they have many times been seen. To hold the belief that angels don't exist would be to deny a lot of data.

Sometimes visions can be faint and elusive. The twenty-minute vision I had as a teenager was for me a one-of-a-kind event, remarkable in its impact on my body and senses. The other visions I have had have been quick and hard to see. Let me try to describe what it's like to see one of these visions. It is almost as if you are looking through glass that has a very faint image on it that is barely visible. Yet at the same time, you can see everything that is beyond the glass. You are simultaneously seeing two different realities. If you make an effort to *focus* on the vision, you become an observer of it. This pulls you out of the visionary experience and into full waking consciousness. Closing your eyes helps block out unnecessary images, but it does not make the visionary image itself any clearer.

The inward nudges we get that give us guidance are usually very subtle and easy to overlook. It is necessary to be very alert for them. We won't be aware of them if our lives are very busy and our minds full of chatter. They are easier to notice when our lives are peaceful, inwardly and outwardly. We can cultivate peacefulness by spending some time every day in prayer and meditation. Mystical experiences do not come through the outer senses. Physical data comes to us through the perceptions of our outer senses. Spiritual data comes through the inner senses. It is as hard to have an inner experience with an outer sense, as it is to hear music with your nose or to taste food with your ears. To use only outer senses and ignore the inner ones greatly limits what can be experienced.

*

In thinking of our lives as merely physical and sensory, we miss much of the essence of humanness. A person is more than just an organized pile of minerals, a living biological being. There is also a very special quality in a person: soul. The Bible calls this "the breath of God." This breath carries with it attributes of God, including the ability to love, to make choices and to create. These make up a sort of spiritual genetic pattern showing that God is the spiritual parent. Each person is a child of God, spiritually.

Each person is uniquely different, spiritually, from every other person. We know that the same two parents can have a lot of children who all look different from each other. And these parents have a fixed, limited number of genes. God, on the other hand, is unlimited. Is it any wonder that each of God's children would be a unique individual? The individual spiritual imprint is called the "image of God." The Bible states that both male and female were created by God in the image of God. This individuated imprint of God is, I believe, a fundamental aspect of the soul. In poetic terms, the Bible tells that God created humankind by making the form out of the "dust of the earth" and then breathing into it the "breath of life." This combination created a *living* soul.

What, exactly, *is* a soul? God knows. The Bible, which is hundreds of pages about the interaction between God and humans, never actually describes either God or the soul. Similarly, the Edgar Cayce readings, which refer to God[9] more than 14,000 times and to the soul 9000 times, never really describe either one. Of course, God is infinite and cannot *be* described. The soul carries the imprint of its maker, the image of the invisible God. The soul is in the image of that which cannot be seen.

Although the soul cannot be seen or described, certain experiences allow a person to feel the presence of the soul within. Though our minds can never really understand the nature of the soul, we can get some sense of how it functions. Each soul is different from every other. It is the person's own self. It is what gives the person individuality. The soul has been called by a variety of names. In the Bible this inner self is sometimes referred to as a person's *heart.* According to some Bible scholars, the word "heart" describes our whole inner being, the central core of mind, emotions and will. Today people are more likely to use the word *soul* to describe the core of our being. The Cayce readings list among the attributes of the soul: consciousness, emotions, and will (the ability to choose). The soul is who we truly are.

The soul is both "dust" and "breath of God," body and spirit. In the soul of each person there is the interpenetration of spirit and body. The soul enables spirit to become embodied. It is our interface with both matter and spirit. Because the soul has God-likeness, we sense our attraction and relationship to God. The soul silently urges us in the direction of spirituality. The soul also allows embodiment of spirit. The nearest we come to "seeing God" is to look at another person. What we do to other people (and to ourselves) we are, in effect, doing to God. In a very basic way, God is present within every person.

*

Sometimes it takes a huge act of faith to believe that God is present in a person whose actions seem to contradict it. Everyone has the ability to plug into the spiritual source, but not everybody does. Each person has been given, by God, the ability to make choices about how to act. By choosing to act in the loving, creative manner that reflects God, an individual comes closer to the experience of his soul's purpose.

Why is it that choices are made in opposition to this harmonious direction? People have lost their awareness that they are children of the living God. They each feel that they are on their own. They feel separate from God and may not even realize God exists. It's not that God really is removed from them. The falling away from God is in *consciousness.* (Separation from God is all in your mind!) God wanted people to be individuals, potential companions. To create the space necessary for us to have free will (choice), God sort of pulled back a little.[10]

The ability to make our own choices is our soul's gift from God. God does not violate it, even when we choose to go against God. The upside of free will is that we are free individuals with the potential to be co-creators and companions to God. The downside is that God allows people to do mean and nasty things to each other, to themselves and to all of creation. It is distressing to us that humans are permitted such freedom that even evil deeds can be done.

Only a few pages into the Bible humans were already so evil that God regretted having made them. "The LORD was grieved that he had made man on the earth, and his heart was filled with pain."[11] Even so, God did not tamper with mankind's free choice and self-determination. Instead, God decided that it would be best to just wipe man and all the other creatures off the face of the earth. Then God decided to leave a few good ones alive (Noah's family.) and give them a chance to make a fresh start. We don't want God to shut the world down. But we want God to make things better somehow. We keep asking God to cut down on other people's choices of action, so that they will act the way we want them to. But that is not something God does.

God does give strength and insight to those who ask so that they can deal with the problems they face. And God can help a person to be in the right place at the right time to gain an advantage. God also enables people to receive personal growth or to benefit from every difficult experience. But this type of help is only for those who decide to be in a personal relationship with God. A relationship is a two-way street. We are more likely to think of what God could do for us than what we could do for God. One thing that anyone could do for God is to express appreciation for being alive. Another is to say something kind to another person, for God's sake.

*

It would be convenient to start life already knowing how to connect to God. One can easily wonder, "If each of us is made of God-stuff, why don't we know it?" Actually, we did know when we were born that we were part of all that is. When we are born we have awareness, consciousness itself, without form or content. As tiny babies we have an *intuitive sense of oneness* with all. Gradually we *learn about separateness.* Around age two, we begin to notice how we are different from everything else. Individuality was true too, from the first moment we became aware. As we became more aware of our personal uniqueness, our awareness of being part of the oneness slipped from our thoughts and into our subconscious. We still have the knowledge of Oneness, but it has been forgotten and needs to be remembered.

I am part of all that is, part of the Infinite Oneness.[12] I am also an individual. I can focus my awareness on either of these aspects of my true nature: my individual existence or my existence within the Oneness. Both are true. To know who I am I need to know myself as myself (an individual) and yet also to know that I am one with God.[13]

Each of us can think and say, "I am." The awareness within me that says "I" is the core of my being; it is "*me*".[14] It is not a part of myself I could step out of without causing serious psychological damage. It is the basis of my consciousness, my capacity for feelings, and my ability to choose. This core of my being cannot be seen. I believe that it is beyond comprehension because it is open-ended to the infinite Oneness. It is the interface between me, as an individual, and me as part of the Oneness of God. We must consider both spirit and matter when we try to know who we are. My inner being touches on both the infinity of God and the particularity of myself.

The Bible says we have been made in God's image. I believe this is so. In God there is the simultaneous existence of Oneness and multiplicity. I used to wonder whether the purpose of my inner being (soul) was to embody Spirit or to spiritualize my body. Now I think both are true, and they are really the same. I make spirit concrete[15] (embodied) by having spiritual purpose for my actions, and that, in turn, makes my life holy (dedicated to God).

I experience my inner abilities intuitively. I feel as if there is a portal in my heart that connects me to the whole universe and all living things. It is my window to insights beyond my own personal experience. Through it God's spirit guides me to live in ways that are truthful, loving and healthy. When I follow this guidance, I feel whole; I feel as if I have come home; I feel that I am being truly me.

Sometimes I think about this 'window' between the infinite and the individual. I imagine it being like a thin film of clear plastic. In the individual who thinks he is better than other people ('hot stuff'), this plastic becomes overheated and draws in on itself, thickening and losing its clarity. By contrast, some people have had such inner clarity that they could even see future events.

The portal in my heart goes two ways. Through it God knows my thoughts, feelings and desires. It is the gatekeeper to the supply line that delivers God's life force and energy into my life. Entirely unobstructed, it could provide the ultimate in life, health and strength.

These images are my metaphors for what I sense but cannot see. They are metaphors for the soul. Like metaphors for God, they represent only particular facets and do not show the whole. Using one of my metaphors for God, I see the soul as a miniature version of the 'cosmic pasta-maker'. I receive life force and energy from the Source. My soul, using its attributes (including, among others, consciousness, emotions, choice and creativity) converts this God-energy into the words and actions. My soul acts in a manner that reflects the formative aspect of God: It takes energy from the one Source and shapes it into a multiplicity of manifestations. When my soul's attributes (mind, feelings, will) are focused on self-inflation, my activities express the energy of God in a distorted way. But this is not the original plan. The true calling of my soul is to make the Spirit available for use by my body and to make my body available for use by the Spirit.

*

I can consciously choose to be a conduit of God's blessings to someone else. Coordinating my words and actions with that intent, I (or anyone else who does it) can be a delivery system of God's love. In this way God's spirit takes solid form. Our hands can become

God's hands, helping to bring wholeness into the world. I believe that when we do this, God's energy literally flows through us to other people. Sometimes when I feel that I am truly doing God's work I have felt a faint sensation, almost like an electrical current, flowing through me. I have noticed that right after helping someone to feel more connected to God, my face glows like the face of someone who has just fallen in love. I have seen other people have this same glow after they had said things that awakened people to awareness of God's presence. I love to help "plug people into God." When I do, I feel more alive and more fully *me* than at any other time. I believe that my spiritual life and physical life are interpenetrating at these times.

Every deed is the manifestation of a thought. When a selfish attitude motivates me, my deeds are self-serving. When awareness of my oneness with God is the impulse for my actions, then my activities advertise the existence of God. When my deeds are the embodiment of God's spirit in me, it is a marriage of spirit and matter. To the extent that I do this, I do my part to help God's "kingdom come on earth as it is in heaven." How can I do this work if I am trying to escape the earth? My purpose here is to impregnate the concrete reality of the world with the oneness of Spirit.

There are a number of ways to marry spirit and matter. A good place to start is by recognizing God's presence in the objects and activities of daily life. My first efforts in this were the childhood prayers I said before eating. That practice gave me brief moments in the day to recognize the food I ate as being a gift from

God. To see God's presence in something makes that thing sacred. The process of shifting the meaning of an object from secular to sacred takes place in the conscious mind. The separation that we have had from God also takes place in the conscious mind. Therefore it is in consciousness that the break must be healed. The separation is due to our own choices in what we think about and, of course, the actions that flow from those thoughts. There is no outside power that can separate us from God.

Another way to help bring heaven on earth is by finding a spiritual purpose for every aspect of life. Since my body is the "temple" in which I interact with God, keeping my body healthy is an important spiritual task. This gives a spiritual purpose to tasks that promote health, including eating, bathing, washing clothes and taking out the trash. Every interaction I have with another person is an opportunity to be a channel of God's love to that person. My appreciation for God's creation is reflected in the ways I show respect for the environment. I can show others how I feel about God by bringing more beauty, happiness, healing and peace wherever I find an opportunity.

If an activity I do awakens in me an awareness of God's presence, then for me that activity has become sacred. When every person becomes aware of being one with God and visualizes the interpenetration of spirit and matter,[16] the whole world will become a sacred place. When all activities are done to reflect God's presence then indeed heaven will be present on earth.

*

Doing my small part to help interpenetrate spirit and matter is totally different from an attempt to withdraw from the world or stamp out my individuality. I did not create my individuality; it is God's gift to me. It is part of my soul. It is the part of my inner being that is aware and active in the physical world. I retain my personal individuality, but join it with the awareness of oneness with God. Then God's presence can live in me in such a way that my activities will testify to God's spirit in me.

Why do I need to bring my individuality together with awareness of oneness with God? How could they have come apart? After all, I am part of creation made of and by God! If God is infinite, why is God not everywhere? If God is in my body, why not in my consciousness? If God is infinite and all-powerful, why are there problems in my life and in the world?

God *is* infinite but has taken on a specific limitation. God has given each of us control over our own consciousness. We have the right to make our own choices. Any choice…including the choice to separate our consciousness from God. Having been born as individuals predisposes us to focus on our individuality. There is nothing wrong with individuality. Individuality is our inner being expressing itself in the world. But it is only half of the function of our inner being. To focus on individuality, over a lifetime, and over generations, results in people forgetting their oneness with God.

*

God is the source of life and love. An individual separated from God is like a plant separated from its roots. A person who is only aware of personal individuality can feel isolated and lonely. He feels that he is his only source of support and protection and may be desperate enough to grab power at the expense of others. The results of this bring fear, pain and grief into personal, community, national and international life. We try to make the world better by punishing and controlling those who do harm to others. But often it feels as if we are trying to stay afloat by bailing out a boat that has a hole in the bottom. No matter how hard we work to correct problems, more arise. The hole needs to be filled. The basic problem is the emptiness within the hearts of individuals. So many of the problems of the world flow from deeds of people with empty hearts. These deeds have consequences that last for generations. People who honestly say, "My life is hell!" may have closed God out of their consciousness. They don't need to live that way. God's presence is everywhere, even in the "depths of hell". People only need to acknowledge God's presence within them to begin the healing. God does not violate anyone's free will, so it is necessary for people to willingly invite God into their consciousness.

We don't need to go anywhere to find God. God has been in us all along, and continues to be in us. We can contact God by going inward. The Bible says that God's law is written in our hearts and that we will find God in a still small voice within.

How does one go "within"? This is not some kind of physical movement. It is a movement of consciousness. It is a change in the contents of awareness. To explore inwardly, is first necessary to learn to stop being aware of what is going on around you. Many people start this first step by focusing all of their attention on their breathing, as an exercise, for a number of minutes each day. As people get better at moving awareness away from outward things, inward experiences begin to open up in their awareness. There is a special kind of excitement, called "quickening", that is felt when moving inward. It is as if you are finding your way home after being lost.

And we have been lost. It is not our bodies that have been lost. It is our consciousness, our awareness that has wandered away from its true home. Until we begin the inward journey we may not realize that that home exists, even if we feel lost, alone or alienated. God did not go away. We, in consciousness, left God.

# Chapter Four: **TAO OF TORAH**

I loved the thrill of extending the limits of my consciousness. I loved the experiences that came as I danced with the infinite. I wanted more. Convinced that God is unlimited, I didn't want my own limitations to block my access to this fountain of blessings. I wanted to travel farther along this road. Where was the roadmap? My friends and family had not traveled this way ahead of me. I was traveling on my own, with no one to give me advice. There could be potholes in the road ahead and I didn't know where they were.

Actually, I thought I might already have fallen into a pothole. A neighbor came over to my house with a ouija board, which she said was a way to get guidance. Now that I knew that there is more to reality than what we meet in daily life, I was ready to experiment. The ouija board did give guidance, but the guidance seemed negative in spirit and I didn't know what source it was coming from. A little later I tried doing automatic writing, which also produced messages, this time claiming to be from my father, who had died. I did not believe that it was Dad because it didn't know the loving nickname that he always called my mother.

While I was doing the automatic writing I had the uncomfortable sensation that someone was behind me, looking over my shoulder at what I wrote. Within days, out of the corner of my eye, I noticed a shadowy figure flash past me. I saw this about once a week for a month. My husband saw it once. Neither of us ever mentioned it to the children. Then, while I was helping my three-year-old wash sand off little tiles we had found on the ground, she said, "Last night I saw a ghost, Mommy." Until that month it had not occurred to me that ghosts might be real, but here was my baby saying she had seen one. I hoped that she had just seen her reflection in the window, or some such, so I asked where the "ghost" had been. She said it had been in the hall, which surprised me since we always left the hall light on at night. I continued the conversation in a casual tone because I didn't want to stir up her imagination.

Was it a man ghost or a woman ghost?
I don't know.
What kind of clothes did it have on?
I couldn't see. It was just peeking in my room.
What did its face look like?
It was kind of airy.

Then what did it do?
It just disappeared.

I was uneasy with the increasing evidence that there was an invisible person in my house. I wanted this person out of my house and didn't know how to make that happen. I wanted to explore beyond the limits of the physical world, but I wanted to do it safely. I didn't want to open doors that led to places I didn't want to be. I needed some instructions.

*

People who spend a lot of time going beyond the physical realm are called mystics. It seemed sensible to read reports of their experiences. Turning first to modern mystics, I attended a meeting where people studied the writings of Rudolf Steiner. A few days later I was with a group that focused on the work of Edgar Cayce. At the close of each of these meetings I asked the people if their studies said anything about automatic writing or ouija boards. At each meeting the answer was the same: "Don't do it. You are opening yourself up to possession". I wasn't sure exactly what this meant, but knew it had something to do with insanity. That's a pretty big pothole!

It was interesting that both of these groups made the same response. Cayce and Steiner were entirely different in many ways. Rudolf Steiner was an Austrian clairvoyant who explored non-physical realities. He called his findings "ethical individualism" and used them as the basis of his philosophy, Anthroposophy. Steiner used his understandings to create innovations in medicine, education architecture and agriculture. On the other hand, Edgar Cayce was an American who never made it past eighth grade. The only book in his home was the Bible. He liked to fish, garden, play games and teach Sunday school. Of the two, I felt more at home with Cayce. I never read any books by Steiner, though I am told that his book *How to Know Higher Worlds* has parallels with my experiences.

Cayce had amazing abilities to predict future events and to accurately diagnose illnesses psychically. He believed this ability was a gift from God. Like me, he was a freelance mystic, exploring the extent of his non-physical abilities without a prepared lesson plan. On a few occasions he fell into potholes, which resulted in some psychic readings that were inaccurate.[17] But the forty-year body of his work taken as a whole provides very helpful guidance on navigating safely in these uncharted waters. Cayce's psychic statements (called *readings*) urge over and over again that all that we do (physically, mentally and spiritually) be directed toward bringing us into harmony with God. I was helped especially by Cayce's information on meditation, prayer, setting ideals and interpreting dreams.

*

Often Cayce's readings sound like quotes from the Bible. The readings illustrate discussions of spiritual growth and psychic development with examples from the Bible. I became curious about whether the Bible could be read as a handbook for psychic development. Cayce read the Bible all the way through sixty-seven times by the time he died at age sixty-seven. He didn't start reading it until he was thirteen so he had to read it multiple times for a number of years to get caught up. I am a slow reader, but I figured that if Cayce could read it sixty-seven times, I should be able to get through it at least once. I had no idea how long it would take. I read for about twenty minutes a day. I fell asleep a few times reading Numbers and Leviticus. But some later chapters were so interesting I lost track of time and read longer than twenty minutes. It took me only nine months to read the whole Bible cover-to-cover.

There is something very peculiar about the Bible. I find that when I read it, insights triggered in my mind answer questions I am wondering about. I read the New Testament straight through about once every ten or fifteen years. Oddly, each time I do, it seems to have material in it that I don't remember reading before. The words are the same, but each time I read the Bible, it speaks to me in a new way. Perhaps this is because I have changed. My understandings are new and in my heart I have different questions than I did when I last read it.

*

When I read the Bible cover-to-cover I saw *connecting to God* as the central theme. The Bible starts out discussing the big disconnect between people and God.

Originally there was only God. All that exists in the universe was brought into manifestation by the activity of God. A sort of kinship exists between God and humans, who are created in a way that reflects God. Right in the middle of God's abundance is the knowledge of good and evil. From the beginning, people have had the ability to make choices. When the choices were self-centered rather than God-centered, people's consciousness began to disconnect from God-awareness. The separation brought pain and hardships into people's lives. Eventually people were being just awful to one another, choosing evil rather than good ways to act. According to the Bible, God tried to resolve the problem by eliminating most people with a major flood. Some survived to make a new start, but things didn't go any better than before. Instead of just ending the whole experiment at that point, God tried a new approach to try to close the gap.

God selected a group of people to use as a demonstration project. They have been known for thousands of years as "the Chosen People" because of being selected for this experiment. But the experiment was not just to benefit the people *in* the experiment (now known as Jews). The purpose was to teach an important lesson to everybody in the world.

God's new approach was to offer people a deal that might make them want to choose to align their will with God's will. The deal was "If you will be my people, and obey my laws, then I will be your God and make good things happen for you." At that time what people wanted most was to win wars, bear children and have good harvests. So that is what God offered. That was God's side of the deal. The people's side of the deal was to obey the laws God gave. The Law is recorded in the Torah, which includes the first five books in the Bible.[18]

*

The laws God put in this deal have a different purpose than laws established by governments. Their purpose is to make a path of action that can help people to have God in their awareness all the time. According to the Law there is a specified godly way to do many of the activities of everyday life. Throughout each day, people are constantly put in the position of choosing to do something the way God specified. The specific requirements of this path are complicated but not remarkable. These include guidelines for everyday life: what to eat, when to wash, what to wear.

The step-by-step living of daily life directed to God helps us reconnect to God. It is interesting that people all over the world describe spiritual life as a walk. The Confucian spiritual path is called Tao, (pronounced "dow"). Tao is translated Way, which reminds me of spiritual walking. The Hebrew word for *law* is related to the word for *walking*. Both the Torah path and the Tao are ways of living. They are paths that become more real by being walked (lived).

Torah is one of the paths that leads to spiritual awareness. "Torah makes possible a path, a way. It tells what can or what should be done. A path with no boundaries is not a path. If a path is important (and Jesus thinks it is), then there has to be some way for you to know when you are off the path."[19] Because there are boundaries (requirements), we know when we have strayed off the path.

I think following rules of behavior for a spiritual purpose can help a person become better connected to God. Constantly using personal will to do God's will can give a person the sense of participating in God's activity. It trains the person to do each activity *for God.* In this way it helps restore God's presence into the individual's consciousness. This works to gradually heal the separation between God and the individual. Separation between people and God comes about through human choice. Even so, God still respects human choice, and doesn't overrule the mistakes we choose to make. So it is up to us to choose to reconnect with God.

*

I never tried following the Torah, but I have taken on other spiritual disciplines. For me, following spiritual disciplines has been a foundation for spiritual growth. A discipline I have followed for many years is to eat foods that I know are good for my body, and avoid the ones that do not promote health. I consider my body to be a temple of God, and so I treat it with respect and try to keep it clean. In my own life it is where I meet God and where we have our interactions. God and I are both always in my body all of the time (though my awareness of this comes and goes.) I try not to trash my body in any way. If I did, I would be showing disrespect for myself as well as for God, and who would benefit from that?

Having this rule for myself gives me a reference point for making decisions in new situations. I once was in Egypt and was able to visit several Egyptian families. The family members spoke little or no English and I spoke no Arabic. Even so, I was made to feel very welcome because Egyptians make great efforts to show hospitality. I was surprised though, when one of my hosts offered me what appeared to be hashish. I never expected this situation to come up in my life. I politely explained to him that it is against my religion. Even though the Bible says nothing about hashish or opium, I knew that to smoke his pipe would violate my own promise to God. Another person in this situation might have made the same choice I did, but for other reasons. There are a number of good reasons to make the decision I made. But I try to have my relationship with God be the *first* reference point I use when responding to a new situation. When I take on a spiritual discipline, it sets boundaries for my behavior. The boundaries I set in my agreements with God help make my decision-making easier. These boundaries are what create the edges of the path I am on. A spiritual path *has* edges; that is what makes it a path. My spiritual path guides my behavior as I walk through life.

A discipline I take on moves my attention away from myself and onto God. Focusing too much on ourselves tends to disconnect us from God. By the very fact that we are individuals, we are tempted to be self-absorbed. We must strengthen the ability to move our attention away from self in order to be able to reach the balance point. We need to see ourselves as individuals. But we also need to see ourselves as connected to God, and therefore connected to everybody else. We find usually ourselves strongly focused on ourselves and on our personal preferences. This needs to be balanced by focus on God.

I experimented once with daytime fasting and found it a powerful means to focus awareness. Some Muslim friends of mine spent a month each year in a religious fast. They did not eat or drink anything during daylight hours, though they did during the dark hours of morning and evening. I had not been introduced to fasting in my church, but I knew fasting had been used for centuries as a spiritual discipline in many religions. So I decided to try it.

For a month I ate a big breakfast before dawn and had no more to eat until nightfall, when I had another large meal. Unlike many Muslims I did drink water during the day, quite a bit of it. I also had a snack before bed, so the amount of food I ate each day was probably near normal. This was not a weight-loss diet designed to alter my appearance. This was a spiritual fast designed to alter my relationship with God. And it did. At the time I undertook the fast, I was a student whose mind easily wandered away from books. I could easily daydream ten minutes here, twenty minutes there, every hour or two. That added up to a lot of lost study time in the course of a day. During the month I fasted this did not happen. I still became distracted from my studies as often as usual. But as soon as my mind began to wander, it wandered to the fact that I was hungry. That would remind me of the fast. As soon as I remembered the fast, I remembered the purpose of the fast: to come closer to God. So I would take a moment to say a prayer. And then I returned to my books. I got a lot more studying done during the fast: in the course of each day I replaced several hours of daydreams with about fifteen minutes of prayer. And I felt closer to God because of being in touch so many times during the day.

It was important that I did not take on that spiritual discipline in hopes of improving my appearance, or to impress anybody. For a spiritual discipline to have a spiritual effect it must have a spiritual motivation. If I have a variety of motivations for a discipline, the spiritual impact in my life will be diluted. And if my true motivation is not spiritual, the discipline won't bring me closer to God, no matter how spiritual it looks!

A discipline sets up a way of behavior that I do over and over. It establishes a pattern that I follow for a period of time. In some instances it is something I intend to do for the rest of my life. When I take on a spiritual discipline, I am making a commitment to God. I remember God's promise: If you will be my people, I will be your God. With the discipline, I am saying by my intent and actions, "Here I am, God, trying to be one of your people." I don't know what response God will make in my life, but I know by experience that it will be nice. I treasure our interactions and want to be sure to keep up my side of the relationship.

*

When I first begin a discipline it is interesting and even a little exciting to do the activity. But after doing the same thing week after week, the excitement wears off. It becomes harder to do the discipline every day. By at least the sixth week, the discipline has become real work. I have to let go of momentary desires in order to keep the commitment I made. I have decided to put God ahead of my personal preferences. The habit of focusing on myself does not easily give way. Though I have had many different kinds of disciplines, I usually come up with the same excuses to avoid the discipline: "I'm unusually tired today"; "This is a silly thing to do"; or "I'm already feeling so spiritually connected today I don't need to do it". This is my self-centered focus yelling for supremacy. I develop new strength by pushing past this resistance. Doing my discipline even when I don't feel like it strengthens my will to choose God. The discipline causes me to grow because it makes me change inwardly. It is easier to connect with God when I learn to detach from the desire to do things according to personal preferences.

There is great variety to the things that people have chosen as spiritual disciplines. For example, some people promise to never have a haircut in their life so that their long hair will advertise their belief in God. But other people promise to always keep their heads shaved as a testimony that God is in charge of their lives. Perhaps the disciplines chosen are not as important as how consistently they are done. Consider the man who keeps his hair long as a testimony to God, to himself, and to other people, that God rules his life. If that man gets a haircut before a job interview, he has put something other than God as his first priority. His action has violated the relationship he has with God. Instead of moving his awareness closer to God, his action increases the gap. Getting a haircut is a spiritual problem for that man because of the spiritual meaning that act has in his life. It is not a problem for a person who has not taken on that discipline. Is a life with no spiritual disciplines a problem-free life? No! We have the big problem of being separated from oneness with God. Spiritual disciplines stimulate us to grow in awareness of God.

A person may be tempted to wonder if he has chosen the "best" discipline. A good discipline is one that you actually do, so that you grow in your sense of connectedness with God. Any discipline, if you did it every day, would become boring or inconvenient. There would be the temptation to stop. When this resistance comes up there becomes the opportunity to overcome self-centeredness. Whenever we choose to be self-absorbed we move farther from awareness of God in us. This problem must be solved by the use of our choice. As we choose to put God first, and make that commitment concrete in actions, the gap closes. A more important question to ask is: Am I doing what I believe God wants me to do? This is important because it puts you into relationship with God. This is at the heart of religious experience. Do you use your own free will to do what you believe God wants you to do?

In God's demonstration project with his chosen

people, God gave the Torah as a tool the people could use to reconnect to God. But over and over the people's consciousness drifted away from God. According to the Bible, this caused God grief. God actually loves everybody. God wants to relate to each one of us. The Oneness, which is God, is cohesive, which is to say… it holds together. Love, connectedness, and wholeness are expressions of this. God misses every single person who wanders off out of relationship with God. The Bible reports God's feelings this way:

> "I was ready to be sought by those who did not ask for me;
> I was ready to be found by those who did not seek me.
> I said, 'Here am I, here am I,'
> to a nation that did not call on my name.
> I spread out my hands all the day to a rebellious people,
> who walk in a way that is not good,
> following their own devices..."[20]

And also this way:

> " "I myself said,
> 'How gladly would I treat you like sons
> and give you a desirable land,
> the most beautiful inheritance of any nation.'
> I thought you would call me 'Father'
> and not turn away from following me.
> But like a woman unfaithful to her husband,
> so you have been unfaithful to me,
> O house of Israel",
> declares the LORD".[21]

*

Instead of moving closer in conscious connection with God, the chosen people along with the rest of humankind drifted farther and farther away. People became more aware of themselves. Consciousness is double edged: I can be aware of unity and wholeness or I can focus on particular individuals such as myself. I can focus on myself as a part of the universe or I can focus on how separate and different I am from everything else. God granted us this freedom when we were created. At the time Torah was given, people generally were less aware of individuality than today. They had a strong sense of themselves as part of nature and as part of a tribe, or group, or nation. This was true in many nations. In Egypt, twenty kings in a row might use the same name.

Intuitive thinking was much more in use at that time. Intuition gives awareness of unity and of spiritual realities. But intuition is not as effective as rational thinking for manipulating the material world and gaining wealth. "Left-brain" rational thinking began to develop around 800 BCE. This was a shift in human consciousness that made people more aware of their individuality. Instead of feeling a part of nature, people began to study nature and to see nature as a thing separate from themselves. This was a major change in consciousness.[22] Looking at nature as an "outsider" made the development of science possible. All of our modern technology grows out of this evolution of consciousness. This new way of thinking made possible the development of medicine, education and the study of history. Even religion was affected. Within 500 years of the rise of this left-brain thinking all of the major world religions made some shift in the direction of logic or classification.

People became more and more aware of themselves as individuals. As I have pointed out, there is a trade-off between being aware of individuality and being aware of Oneness, so it has affected the way people relate to God. The trend toward individuation gained increasing momentum as the years went by, and moved fastest and farthest in the West. By the close of the Twentieth Century many people had separated from family, friends, neighbors and spouse during the course of their life. A sense of connectedness to other people fell away, along with the awareness of connectedness to God. Science and technology became the power of the Twentieth Century. In place of God, humankind turned to science (which is to say, humankind turned to itself) to be saved from harm. Within their hearts humans trusted human power more than they trusted the power of God. (To replace God with *anything* is a serious spiritual mistake.) But life, which was expected to get better and better, instead got more dysfunctional, filled with tension and random violence. People shifted back and forth between feeling all-powerful and getting depressed by a sense of hopelessness. People became more anxious in an increasingly broken world. Having lost awareness of God, people expected themselves to do what they were powerless to do.

*

Consciousness evolves slowly. Left-brain thinking developed for about 2500 years before people began to realize its limitations. This type of thinking gave humans greater power to create and increased their self-awareness. God allowed this change in consciousness even though it increased the separation between God and God's loved ones. But God helped people to rediscover their divine connection even under these new conditions. (God meets each person in a way that can be understood by that person.) People, aware of themselves as individuals, began realizing that they could relate to God in a *personal* way.[23]

Before this, religious practices purified entire groups rather than individuals. When Torah was given as a path to oneness, people had more of a group consciousness than we do today. Torah is a path designed to create a holy *group* of people. As people began thinking of themselves as individuals, they realized it was possible to be holy as an *individual.* This prepared them for new understandings about God. Some of these new understandings can be found in the words of the Jewish prophets who lived during this time of changing consciousness. For example, Micah declares that what God requires of people, rather than any material sacrifice, is to "to act justly and to love mercy and to walk humbly with your God." This personal or individual path to God involves both outward actions (justice) and inner attitudes (love). Micah considers humility to be very important. I do too, and I will talk about it in the last chapter.

The development of an individual path to God did not eliminate the validity of the group path. We are individuals, but we continue to live in groups. God wants to connect with us regardless of which path we take. Mystical paths to God have developed in many religions. These largely interior paths tend to appeal to intuitive people. They exist as options among the many ways to connect to God. They do not replace action-oriented or group religious practices. The mystical path that developed in Judaism, called Kabbalah, did not eliminate the validity of the Torah as a route to connection to God. The Torah path is a testament to the importance of making spiritual intentions concrete in words and actions.

*

God continually tries to get us to wake up and reconnect our lives to the love and oneness of God. God, it seems, will do just about *anything* to get this message across to us. Finally (by the grace of God) there was an actual prototype, a concrete example of the embodiment of God in human life. This was a further step in revealing the truth about the human-to-divine connection. The truth itself had not changed. It had been the same since humanity began. In part, what was changing was the level at which the truth was understood. The first contract ("covenant") in the Bible was an agreement made between God and a group of people, the Jews. This agreement still continues to be in effect. (Even the Catholic Church realizes that!) But when people had become more aware of themselves as individuals, a new covenant became possible. This is the contract between God and an individual.

This remarkable event once again involved some of God's chosen people, especially a Jew named Jeshua ben Joseph. Jeshua was born to a Jewish mother, Miriam. She risked death by stoning to begin the pregnancy in the way she understood to be the will of God. Her husband also made personal sacrifices to God's will, including taking his family to live as refugees in a foreign country for a number of years. They were observant Jews who had their infant son circumcised. When they were back in their own country, they went each year to Jerusalem for Passover.

The earliest accounts of Jeshua were written in Greek, and that is why he is most commonly known by the Greek version of his name, which is "Jesus". He did not speak Greek, so I use the Hebrew translation: Jeshua. Some prefer to use "Joshua". Hebrew doesn't have any vowels, so you can use whichever vowels you prefer. Two thousand years ago people did not have last names. They might be referred to as being someone's son or daughter. "Ben Joseph" means "son of Joseph". A modern English version of his name could be "Joshua Josephson".

Jeshua had great aptitude for Torah study. There is no mention in the Bible concerning his education or the years between ages 12 - 30. Then he began his three-year career as a traveling Jewish spiritual teacher. Although it did not make him unique in his own time, he did impressive miracles and healings, including bringing dead people back to life. He said that people who have faith in him would be able to do all the things he did, and even more after his return to the Father.[24] Some of Jeshua's followers did do faith healings and even brought someone back to life. Today, however, where "scientific laws" are held in higher regard than the belief in God, such attempts are not made.

*

Jeshua gave moral teachings, mostly drawn out of the Torah and the words of the prophets. Among these teachings was an emphasis on loving God with every aspect of one's self: with soul, with mind, with heart, with strength. He also taught that it is important for us to wish for good for other people as much as we wish it for ourselves. Jeshua especially taught people to forgive each other and to avoid judging other people. He preached a reverse of the value of social status, saying that God prefers the people who society values least. Jeshua considered God to be a father to him, and to other people as well. He recommended that his friends direct their prayers to "our father in heaven". He was criticized for claiming God as his father. He responded by quoting a Bible verse that says that we are all sons of God. He urged people to recognize that they are indeed children of God. He spoke often of the importance of working toward being in the kingdom of heaven, which was not the *location*, but the *quality* of someone's existence.

Jeshua had a wide vision of spirituality, seeing that

the motivations for a person's actions may be even more important than the acts themselves. This was a new emphasis in the tradition of the Chosen People, but it had the same goal of connecting people with God. It was still a path helping a person to have Spirit interpenetrate material life. And there was still a way to know if you had gotten off the path. But what marked the edges of the path was different. In the Torah, the path was marked by deeds that should or should not be done. Spirit, rather than rules, marked the edges of the path that Jesus taught. Actions needed to be in compliance with God's Spirit. If the spirit (motivation) of the action was in tune with God's Spirit, then it wasn't necessary to use the Law's rules to judge actions. But Jeshua told people that if they did not live in compliance with the Spirit, they should follow the Law of Torah. Whether we live under the Law or the Spirit, it is important to interpenetrate spirit into our lives and consciousness.

Inward and outward paths are not as separate as I may have made them sound. Following an outer path will affect a person inwardly, and an inward journey will affect the way a person lives. If a person is aware of inner feelings and emotions, spirit needs to interpenetrate these areas. We need to invite God into *all* that we think, feel, and do. Whether living under the Law or under the Spirit, the point is to live in a way that brings spirit and matter together in consciousness.

*Thinking* about uniting spirit and matter isn't enough, however. Spirit and matter need to be integrated in our actions too. Jeshua said that the deeds a person does shows what is in that person's consciousness. Doing deeds that tie spirit to matter heals the sense of brokenness that lies deep in our hearts. Spirit and matter need to come together in *consciousness*, because it was in our conscious awareness that they became separated. Our deeds themselves need to be done for a spiritual purpose (which is quite different from asking for a spiritual blessing on them after we have done them). Jeshua told his followers to live under the Spirit but also that that spirit needed to be manifested in actual deeds. I think the way of living Jeshua proposed could be described as "religion of concrete spirit."[25]

Jeshua referred to himself as *fulfilling the law*. He showed what the interpenetration of spirit and matter could look like in an actual test case. Jeshua's personal willingness to do God's wishes certainly was essential. He had free will like the rest of us and could choose whether or not to live his life as he did. Jeshua was the first to actually get it together, and he was willing even to sacrifice his life for other people to do it. He embodied the integration of spirit and matter. He hoped the rest of us would follow his lead, choosing to help God's will to be done in actual deeds. I think that interpenetration of spirit and matter was God's plan for all people from the beginning of time. The pattern has existed eternally. Insights about how to do it have come to people around the world. Jeshua became a living example. This was further unfolding of God's plan. God became as near and concrete to people as a living, interacting person. Step by step, God becomes increasingly present to us.

Jeshua was an individual fully interpenetrated by Spirit. This concept is available now to the general public. We recognize that there has been an actual person whose life was fully dedicated to spiritual purpose. Individuality and Oneness existed simultaneously in the same person, so we know it is possible. Now the concept exists. It can be talked about and attempted. Jeshua set an example for us. We can try to live as he did, with our lives fully interpenetrated by God's Spirit. The catch is that we can't do it on our own. Jeshua couldn't either. He said, "By myself I can do nothing..."[26] He was able to have his life be an expression of God's love because he was empowered by God.

He manifested this pattern entirely, giving his life to do it. Bringing together spirit and matter within his consciousness and actions, Jeshua became the vehicle God used to create a change in the human relationship to God. All of us are able to open ourselves to being "filled" (energized, strengthened, healed) with God's spirit. But God's morphing aspect that had created and shaped the universe was somehow able to fuse with an individual. The formative principle formed itself. To take solid form, it was necessary to exist in a specific time and place. It occurred in Israel in the individual, Jeshua. I am not sure how it happened. A lot of people believe that Jeshua was fully interpenetrated with divinity and humanity at the time of his birth, though the Bible doesn't actually say so. Since it is typical of humans to not be born with fully developed egos, it seems reasonable to me that Jeshua could have become increasingly aware of Oneness with God as he matured. Some Bible scholars think that the interpenetration may have occurred in stages at various points in his life, though they all agree that during at least part of his lifetime Jeshua was fully divine simultaneously with being fully human.

The formative aspect of God involves much more than the three dimensions of our world, so I do not think it is humanly possible for us to understand what it is. We would love to know how it came to interpenetrate the individual life of Jeshua, but I doubt that our human minds are capable of perceiving that. What we need to understand is how *our* lives are affected by this occurrence in which God's morphing ability interpenetrated specific individuality.

Because his individuality had become one with an eternal pattern, the union he achieved of body and spirit became more than just a one-time occurrence. The pattern of interpenetration Jeshua had embodied continued to exist after his death. The individual, Jeshua, is united with the unlimited, the Infinite. We name this interpenetrated pattern with the Greek words "Jesus Christ". When we use this interpenetrated pattern ourselves, divine energy is more accessible to us. In this way, God made it easier for us to interpenetrate spirit in our lives.

*

This marriage of interpenetration of Spirit and matter became a pattern available by request. If we become patterned in this way, it opens access to an unlimited source of healing energy and emotional support. Our access is limited only by our own beliefs. If you act in loving kindness toward other people, it is possible for this pattern to stay in you. The pattern is available to anyone, but the pattern enters you only if requested. God respects your free will. You have to want to have spirit and matter joined within you. The separation between you and God can be bridged. It is a matter of choice: your choice.

What is this pattern we can request? In its accessible form it meets us in its individuated form, as Jesus. But even though it (he) shows up in human appearance, the laws of physics do not limit him. Jesus' body is reported to have dematerialized a few days after he died. It could appear and disappear, move through solid objects like a door, or become solid enough to eat a meal. This may sound like fantasy, but the people who first saw these things were so impressed that they became willing to face execution for talking publicly about it. Jesus has continued to appear, even to the present time. Like many other people, I know this from personal experience.

One day I was expecting company to arrive at 2:00. I finished my house cleaning and other preparations with ten minutes to spare. Ten minutes isn't long enough to start another project, but it is too long to do nothing.

So I used the time for meditation and prayer. I soon found myself partly in an altered state of consciousness. I was still aware that I was sitting in the chair with a window behind me, and that people would soon arrive. But in my mind I heard the fanfare of trumpets as if a king was being announced. I knew with certainty that the Most High was being announced. I wondered whether the trumpets were announcing God or Christ. Then I wondered if the fact that I was hearing it meant that I would come into the Presence. Wow! What an awesome experience that would be! Then it began to feel more and more likely that this experience was going to happen to me. I wondered what a person is supposed to do in the presence of the Most High. It seemed that there must be some way to act in the Presence. I got a little anxious because I had no idea how to act. I thought, "If I were a Catholic or Episcopalian, I'd kneel. If I were Baptist I'd probably stand up. If I were Muslim I would lie face down on the floor. But I'm a Congregationalist and we don't have any protocol about how to act with God." There was no more time to think. It was happening. In my mind I stood up, though I could tell that my body was still sitting down. Suddenly Jesus appeared, wearing a shirt and jeans. His long hair was tied with a hippie headband. He gave me a big smile and clapped me on the shoulder like a dear friend. He said, "I just want to be your friend!" and instantly disappeared. I was stunned. Then I was moved simultaneously to tears and laughter. I think he appeared in hippie clothing to poke fun at my concern about finding some "proper" way to act in God's presence. God's presence isn't just for special occasions. God wants to be in our consciousness all the time. I needed to be in a more familiar relationship with God. I need to be who I really am and be in God's presence at the same time.

*

There is now a bridge between materiality and Spirit because Jesus, fully individualized and fully physical, is now fully spiritual. He predicted that because this is now the case, people who believe it will be able to do what he did and even more. One way to get into this consciousness is to earnestly want to be able to do what Jesus did (manifesting Spirit in deeds). Even just calling on the name of Jesus[27] can empower someone who uses it while accepting the reality of what it represents. I can't explain this but I have experienced it myself. I know other people who have had this experience too. Some of them did not consider themselves "Christians" and were surprised by the power they found in the Name of Jesus. I have relied many times on the presence of Jesus to interpenetrate my consciousness (and therefore my activity) with Spirit. I think it might be possible for someone who was unfamiliar with Jesus to reach this bridge by desiring to become a manifestation of universal love. In any case, I believe it is this *cosmic reality of interpenetrated Spirit and matter* that gets everyone across the bridge, even those who are unaware of the Name by which it is known to many.

Jesus showed a pathway into oneness. God has shown pathways to oneness in various times and places.

The pathways differ, but they all go to the same doorway: full interpenetration of spirit and matter (Interpenetration is *full* when it is *lived*). It is the pattern that formed matter from oneness in the beginning. It is this same pattern through which the multiplicity returns to awareness of Oneness. Anyone who manages to attain the full interpenetration of spirit and matter has reached the door to Oneness. No matter what pathway gets a person to that door, that person has attained "Christ consciousness" and has returned to the Father (God).

It is very difficult to break the limitations created by our individuality. In the mystical experience I had when I was a teenager, this struggle was very clear. No matter how determined I was, I did not have enough strength to get all the way to God-centeredness. With a touch as light as a feather, Jeshua as Christ, the Pattern of Interpenetration, brought me into God-centeredness. The Pattern of Interpenetration is universal. Anyone may call on it.

## Chapter 5: **INTERPENETRATION**

Words always fall short of explaining spiritual reality. Pictures fall short, too. I have been using words to try to explain my thoughts on interpenetrating spirit and matter. Now I will try using illustrations. I hope that you will be able to go beyond the limitations of my words and pictures to deeper understanding.

## ONENESS

Before the beginning of time
there was nothing but infinte Oneness
which we call
GOD.

There is no picture on this page because
until the universe was created
there was nothing visible.
There was only GOD, which is spirit.

# CREATION

Some of the Oneness morphed into multiplicity.
This is how atoms came to exist,
and all that is in the universe that is made of matter.

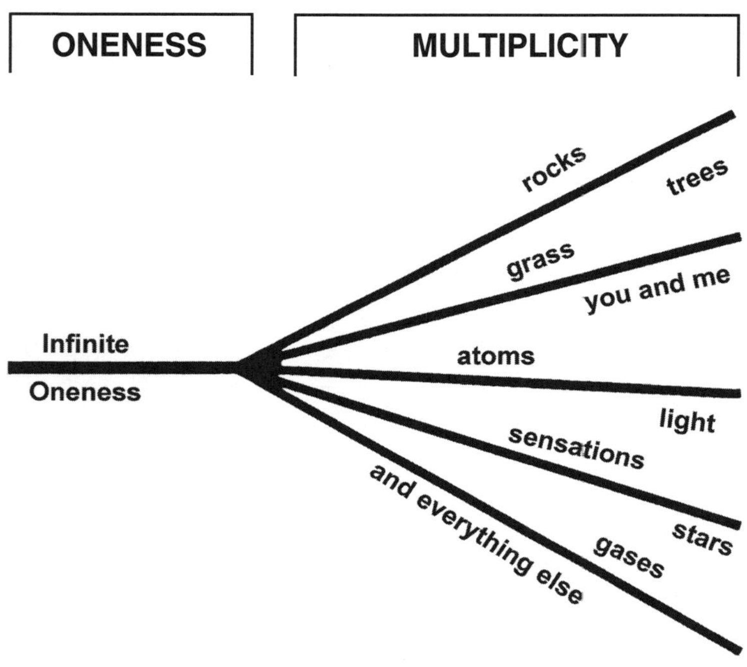

Like everything else that has been created,
our bodies are made of matter formed of
infinite spirit.

We are expressions of God in the material world.

We can be aware of ourselves as individuals
or we can be aware of ourselves as unique
crystallizations of Oneness.

God is represented as both the dough and the noodles.
God is also the pasta machine
that forms the dough into individual shapes.
God is the widsom and power that runs the machine.
God is infinite.
Nothing limits God.
There is nothing outside God.
God is all that is.

## COSMIC PASTA MAKER

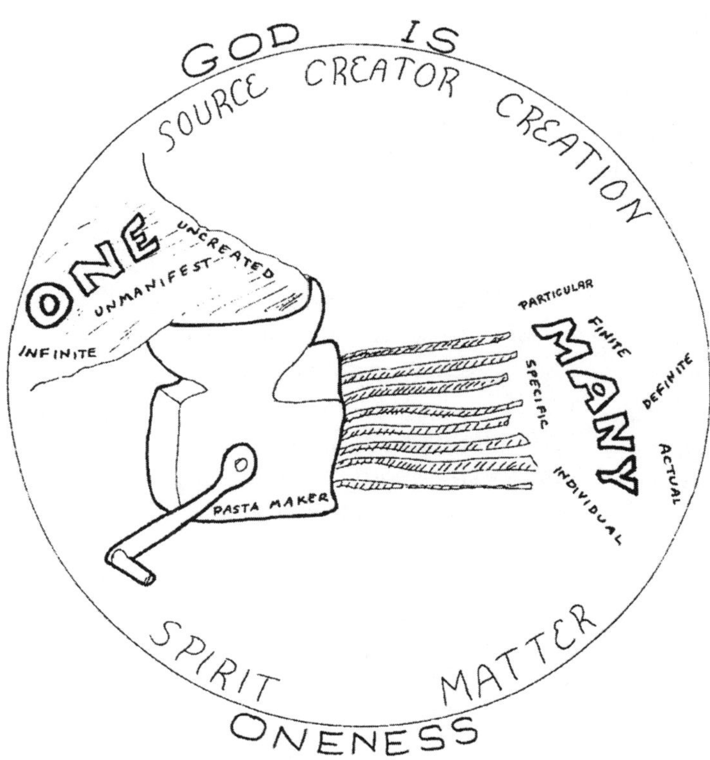

GOD is aware of us
and desires relationship with us,

But we are rarely aware
of our relationship with God.

We focus on our individual lives.
We think about material things,
and we desire to possess them.

## GOD FOCUSES ON US
## BUT WE FOCUS ON THINGS

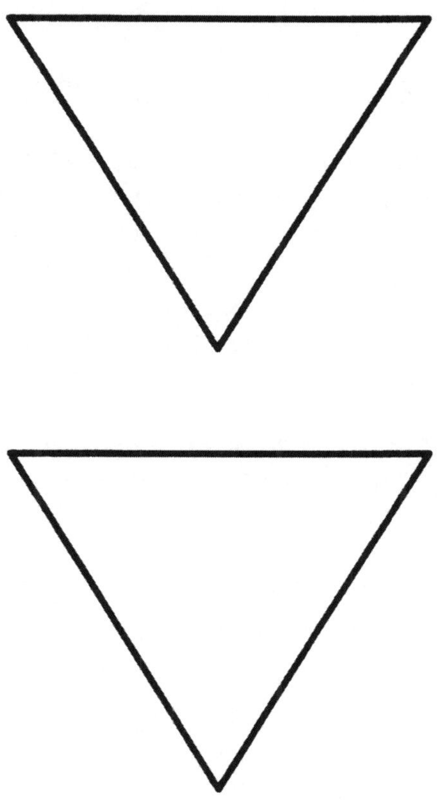

## FALLING AWAY FROM ONENESS

Spirit is one, cohesive and whole.
Spirit gives outward, as with open hand.
It never abandons what it has birthed.

Senses invite us into the world.
Feeling so good, we grab all we can.
We grasp. We hold on. We want to be great.

So busy with all our possessions
We do not know God reaches toward us.
We forget God. We focus on ourselves.

*"...I was ready to be found by people who weren't looking for me. I said,*
*'Here I am! Here I am!*
*...and reached out my hands..."*

- God
(As quoted by Isaiah)

# I WILL GET UP OUT OF THIS MUCK AND RETURN TO MY FATHER

A Story by Jesus

*A young man convinced his father to give him what he was going to inherit. When he got the money, he moved to another country. He corrupted his life, and used up all the money on prostitutes. When he ran out of money there were severe food shortages through the whole country. He couldn't get anything to eat. He got a job feeding pigs and wished he could eat their food. Being jealous of pigs shocked him so much that he came to his senses. He remembered that all the people who worked for his father had plenty to eat. The young man realized that his father might disown him. But he started home anyway, to ask for a job. When he got near home, his father saw him in the distance and ran to meet him. The son began apologizing, but his father interrupted to order clean clothes and jewelry for his son to wear. The father arranged a big party to celebrate, saying, "This is my son who was dead, but now he is alive! He was lost and now he is found!*

If we are really sorry, God is a very forgiving father. No matter where we have been, he wants us to come home.

## AWAKENING

The moment of awakening is
the beginning of the spiritual journey

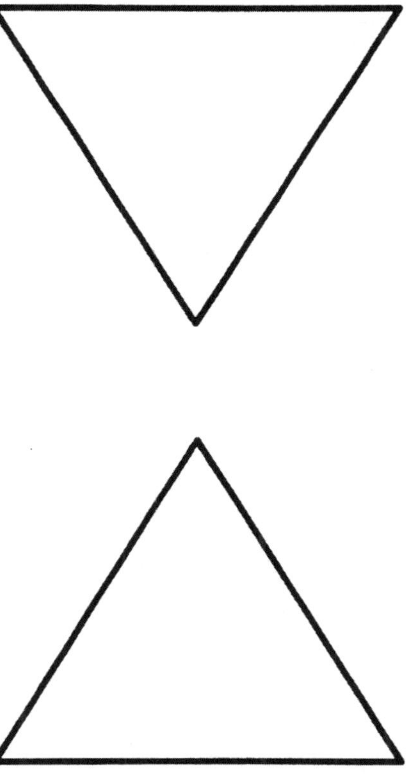

When we realize that our physical experiences and material possessions do not bring true happiness, we can say in the words of the Prodigal Son, "I will get up and return to my father." We can return our awareness to our oneness with God.

## A PERSON'S FIRST CONSCIOUS AWARENESS OF SPIRIT

This is the moment people first realize
that God can be part of their lives.
For many it feels like they are "coming home."
I think they are waking up to awareness of their own
soul, the connector of body and spirit.

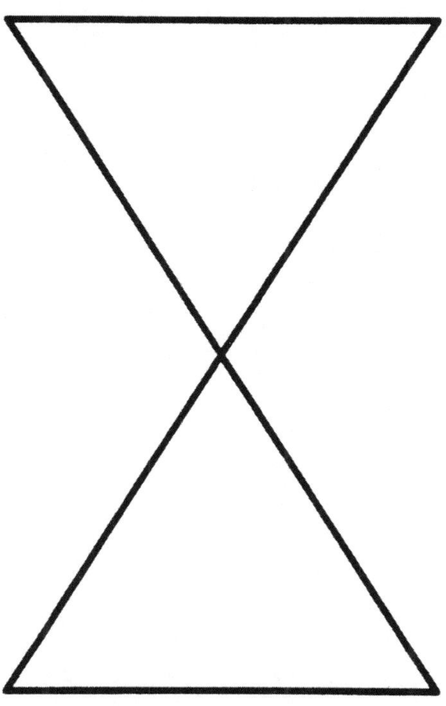

## INTERPENETRATING SPIRIT AND BODY

When we have spiritual reasons for the things we do, our daily lives connect with God. As spirit interpenetrates our material lives, goodness flows through us to other people. The more that spirit and matter overlap in our lives, the more good deeds we do.

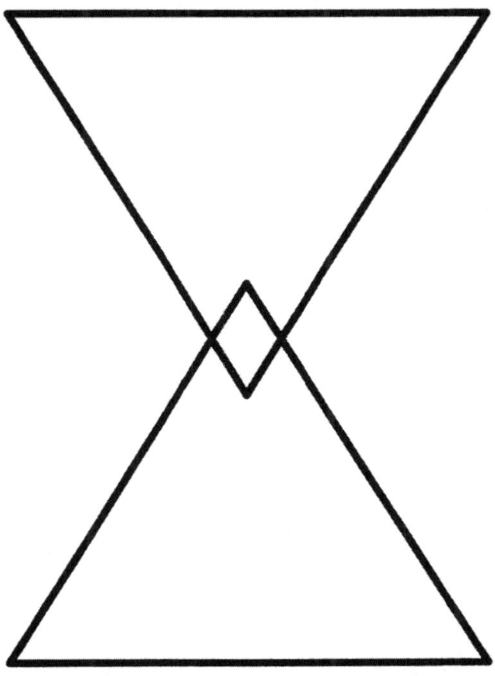

## THE LIGHT SHINES OUT

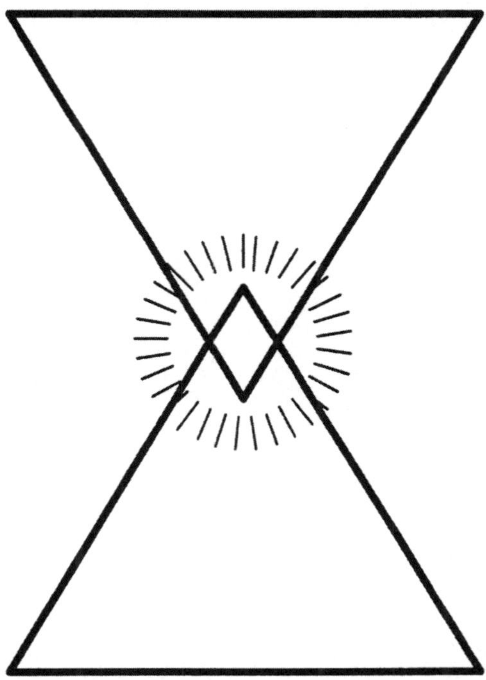

The light of God shines into the world in the good deeds we do. When people see our good works, they are seeing God's action in the world.

God deserves some of the credit when our deeds have been empowered by spirit.

## A LIFE WELL LIVED

The more spirit and matter interpenetrate in our lives, the more light of God that can shine through us. Some very wonderful people interpenetrated spirit and matter in large parts of their lives. Jesus fully interpenetrated spirit and matter in his life.

## FULL INTERPENETRATION

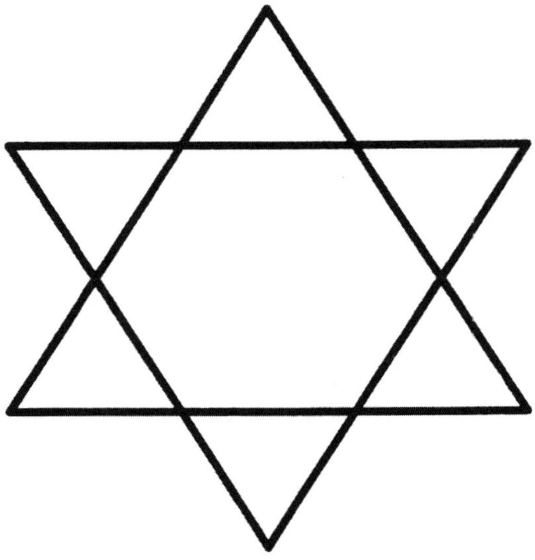

The full interpenetration of spirit and matter is the principle that underlies all of creation.

This "blueprint of the universe" has been called TORAH in the broadest meaning of that word (*See:* Note 18).

Even though a natural law has existed throughout time, science often names the law after the first person who describes it.

The pattern of full interpenetration of spirit and matter is an eternal law.
This law was fully understood and lived by Jesus Christ.

This is why interpenetrating spirit and matter in all areas of life can be called
CHRIST CONSCIOUSNESS.

In the next illustration, the star formed by the interpenetrated triangles reminds us that Jesus was Jewish. The Taoist yin-yang symbol represents the coincidence of opposites that comes with interpenetration of spirit and matter. It also reminds us of the importance of balance. The Islamic decorations carry the understanding that God is far more than the spiritual presence in us. God is unknowably infinite and therefore can never be truly described or pictured.

## UNIVERSAL PATTERN

Christ Consciousness is a universal truth.
It does not just belong to one religion.
It is possible for anyone.

When we have Christ Consciousness,
our actions reflect who we are as individuals
and also the realization that we are one with God.

## ETERNAL PATTERN

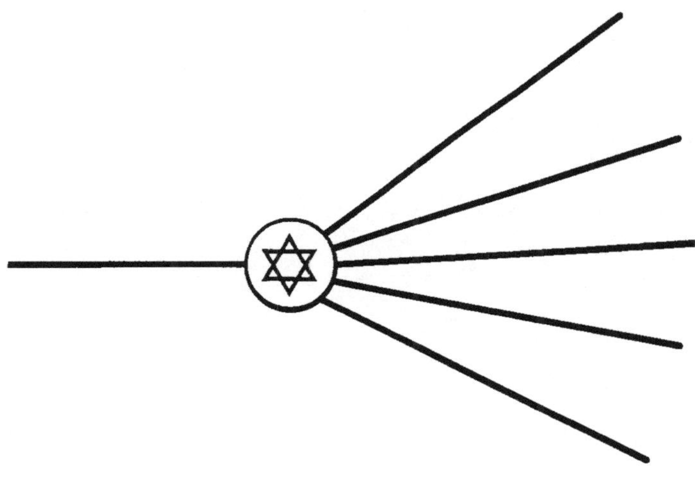

This pattern of interpenetrated spirit and matter is an eternal pattern. It is the fundamental truth of the universe. It is sometimes called Logos or the Word of God. I believe that it is through this truth that spirit morphed into materiality. All that was created is an expression of the spirit that formed it.

## DOORWAY TO GOD

There are a number of ways that we can learn that is important to bring spiritual purpose into our lives. A person who truly understands (and lives) interpenetrated spirit and matter has returned in consciousness to the wholeness and harmony of God.

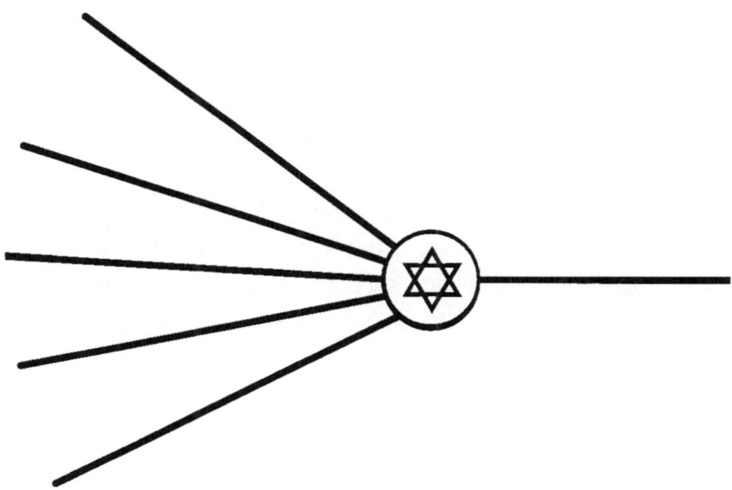

Any person whose life interpenetrates
spirit and matter is present to God.
Living interpenetrated spirit and matter
is the doorway into God's presence.

There are many pathways to that doorway.
Following the example set by Jesus in the
way he lived leads directly to that doorway.
God can guide people to that doorway
by other pathways, too.

# PATHWAYS TO THE DOORWAY

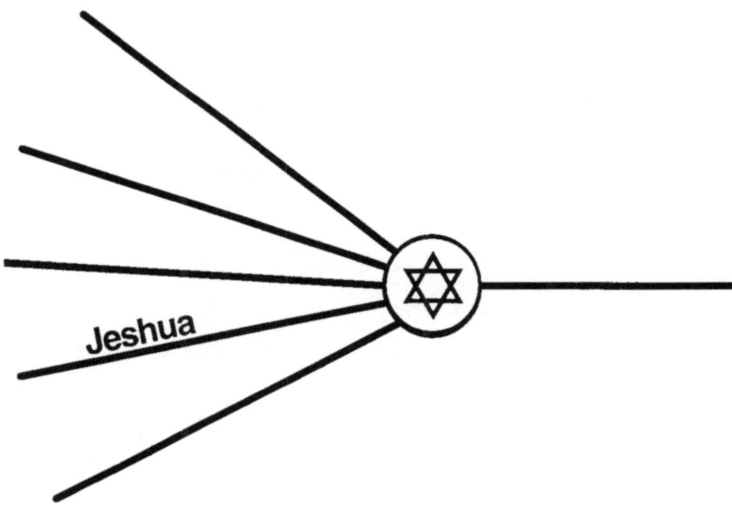


When Jesus said, "I am the way to God," I believe he spoke of the eternal, formative pattern (the Logos) manifested in his life. The pattern did not begin when Jesus was born. It existed even before the beginning of time. It is the eternal truth of interpenetrated spirit and matter.

*Love the LORD your God with all your heart*
*and with all your soul*
*and with all your strength.*
- Moses

*He has showed you, O man, what is good.*
*And what does the LORD require of you?*
*To act justly and to love mercy*
*and to walk humbly with your God.*
- Micah

*'Love the Lord your God with all your heart*
*and with all your soul and with all your mind.'*
*This is the first and greatest commandment.*
*And the second is like it:*
*'Love your neighbor as yourself.'*
- Jesus

Selections from the *Holy Bible, New International Version:* Deuteronomy 6:5; Micah 6:8; Matthew 22:37-39.

## ENTERING ONENESS WITH GOD

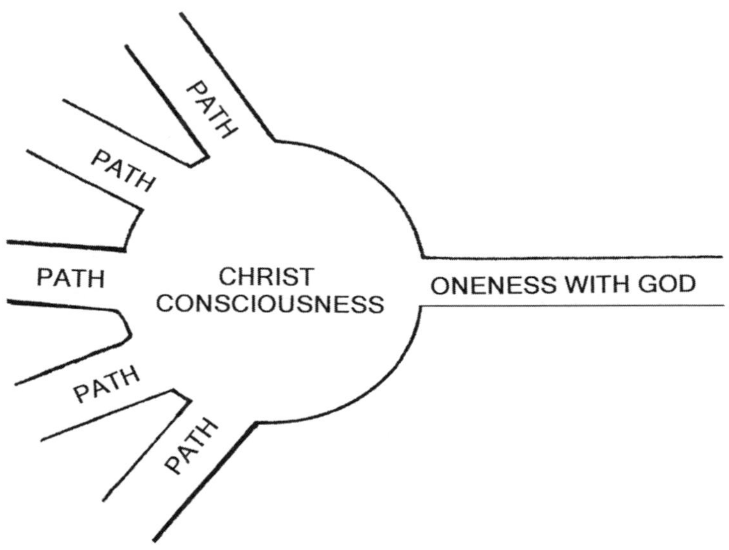


Christ Consciousness includes focus on God, caring as much for others as for self, and humility.

These things can only be done with God's help, and it is necessary to ask God for this help.

Christ Consciousness comes to those who truly want it and who ask in the name of Jesus Christ.

Accepting this consciousness changes life.

# SPIRITUAL JOURNEY'S DESTINATION: WHOLENESS

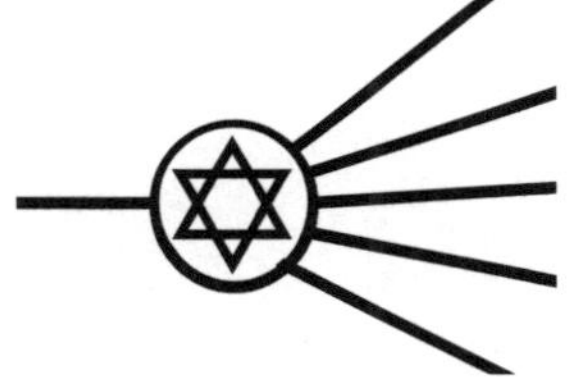

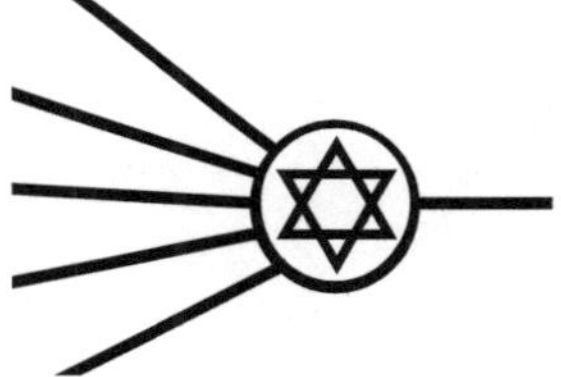

Interpenetrated spirit and matter
is the origin and also the goal
of life on earth.

## Chapter Six: **CONCRETE SPIRIT**

Many times I have wondered about the details of how God and human united in the life of Jesus. One time when I was deeply focusing my attention on this question, I saw a powerful vision in which the image was blurred. It extended way past the edges of my visual screen and was too bright to look at. It was an explosively quick vision, leaving me with the sense that it was a question I shouldn't even ask. I had another vision similar to this. At the time I was wondering about the nature of the soul; how spirit and body connect within us. The vision did not vibrate as fast, but even so it was too fast to see clearly. The form was somewhat like a human's shape, but the edges were indistinct and blurred as if from rapid movement. I was reminded of the blades of a fan, when their movement is nearly fast enough for them to disappear from sight. Only edges of the blades are visible, and they move too fast to be counted. A person looking at a fan going this speed might think there were fifty blades instead of three or four. As I looked at the vision, it was vibrating too fast for me to see clearly. My hunch is that the soul vibrates at a frequency that the human mind is unable to perceive. Our minds are designed to work with the physical world, but the soul is more than physical. Even in the physical world there are bands of colors our eyes can't see and sound frequencies our ears can't hear. I think there are details about the soul and about Christ that we cannot know…not because they are secret, but because they are unknowable.

The similarity of these two visions reminds me of the similarity between the materialized Logos (Christ) and the soul itself. Each makes possible the interaction of spirit and matter. While the soul establishes this interface within a single individual, Christ provides an improved connection that is available to anyone in the world.

Having said this much about the nature of soul and of Christ, I wonder if I should have said anything at all. The Bible does not describe souls or the resurrected Christ, and probably for a very good reason. To think *about* something requires putting some distance between myself and the thing I am thinking about. It would be a big mistake to distance myself from my soul! Awareness of connection of my body and spirit is something I want to increase, *not* decrease! To speculate about the connection between my body and spirit ironically moves me farther from the connection. I need to *live* the connection, not think about it. Christ did not leave his followers with a list of things to think about; he told them to do loving acts of kindness. In this way they would be living the pattern he had set. Their lives would be expressing spiritual values. Spirit and matter would interpenetrate in them.

*

I think that unifying body and spirit is the greatest challenge and most enjoyable experience a soul can have. This is what Christ Consciousness is all about. Jesus was aware of his oneness with God. And he lived it out. His deeds were demonstrations of God's spirit. He recommended this lifestyle to his followers too. He gave them only one command, which was to love and care for other people. He said that if they did that, they would experience God's presence in themselves. To have the mind of Christ is a way of acting, not just a way of thinking. Christ Consciousness becomes fact when it is lived, when it solidifies into words and deeds.

My body feels harmonized with God's spirit when my actions are rooted in my spiritual values. I know it would be good to do this all the time, but I haven't been as successful at mixing body and spirit as I would like to be. I may have gained some understanding of the reasons for this by thinking about what it means to "mix". To make dough out of flour and water, I have to mix *two* things: flour *and* water. It is obvious that I can't mix them together if I only have the flour but no water, or if I have water but no flour. The same is true about mixing spirit and matter. Both need to be present in order for them to combine.

I used to assume that body and spirit were available in my life and ready to be mixed. But I was only partly right. Body and spirit were both *present* in my life, but not necessarily *available*. Sometimes I have difficulty connecting with God. This is not because God has left me, but because my consciousness has left God. When I try to *think* about God I am mentally standing apart from God in order to be "objective". Unfortunately this "standing apart" moves my consciousness away from God. No wonder it is hard to connect! There have also been times when I blocked God's spirit with the belief that my body or mind weren't pure enough. I thought I needed to be all cleaned up before I could invite God in. Believing that God cannot, will not, or should not enter my life blocks the flow of spirit in my life, almost like putting a cork in a bottle.

There are other people who seem to have problems with this too. I know a woman who felt that she could never connect with God because she would never be worthy. She heard discussion of "unworthiness" at church when she was little. It gave her the idea that God wouldn't want to mix with her. God is holy. Yes! But that does not prevent God from entering into a broken, misused human life. That is exactly what God wants to do. If we believe that God does not want to be invited by us, we put a large and unnecessary boulder in our spiritual path. It shuts God out of our lives because God does not enter without permission. We keep God out by believing that God would not want to enter.

We have the key to the door. If we will open the door, God will enter. So when I want to mix body and spirit, spirit is available unless I have blocked it by believing a lie. Spirit is one of the two ingredients I need to mix. The other is my body, my life.

If spirit is the water in my dough, my body is the flour. How much flour will I put in the dough? How much of my life am I willing to mix with God? Will I mix God's spirit with how I spend money? Or how I *make* money…how I choose my friends…what I say when I'm tired and irritable…what movies I watch. Like a friendship, my intimacy with God grows the more of myself I share. I can invite spirit to enter my life more deeply by being aware of God's spirit as I look at my motivations, fears and regrets. (And once they are in the mix they can be healed.) Am I willing to share with God all that I *have* been and all that I *can* be?

*

I can't unlock the door of my heart to God's spirit unless I think I have the keys. I can't give God permission to enter my life unless I believe that I am in charge. This can be really hard for people who are used to being pushed around by other people. Even though many years ago I wanted to give my life to God, I couldn't give what I didn't own. Some of the most important steps I took at the beginning of my spiritual journey were in the direction of coming to claim myself as an individual. God had given me the right to choose, but I was reluctant to make choices. I was afraid I might make the wrong decision and felt safer if I followed choices someone else made. I foolishly thought that if the choice turned out to be a mistake I could get out of responsibility for it because it had been someone else's idea. Now I realize I am responsible for all the things I do even if I have chosen someone else's plan. The consequences that come are my very own.

Making choices is the basis of spiritual growth, in my opinion. The ability to make choices is a gift from God and is what makes me individual. I have learned to claim this ability and I try to use it spiritually. There are many people in the world who like to control other people. I am not referring just to dictators or cult leaders. It is easy to find friends and relatives who like to tell other people how to live. I have been at both ends of this; I have been pushed around quite a bit, but I have also pushed other people into doing what *I* wanted. Neither is a good place to be. Since making choices is such an essential part of the journey to God it needs to be protected and treated with great respect. Part of my journey has been to learn how to avoid being pushed around and how to resist pushing other people around.

It is good for people to make their own choices. Something that is a good choice in one person's life might not work out so well in another person's life. We are all different, in terms of our emotions, life experiences and even our biochemistry. There is a lot we don't know about ourselves and even more that we don't know about other people. Only God knows everything. But we often forget that and try to push each other into doing what *we* think is best. The ability to choose what to do is a precious gift God gives me, along with life itself. I appreciate it. I will defend it throughout my life because it makes possible my journey into God. We have to claim our right to make our own decisions. (Maybe that is God's purpose in making the teenage years a part of our lives.)

*

Often influences on us are hard to notice. I am convinced that the feelings of people nearby can soak into us, even if the feelings are not mentioned. This may be why it feels more exciting to watch sports in a crowd than to see the same game when sitting alone at home. It is easy to share feelings of a crowd that is celebrating, or a crowd in a shopping frenzy, or a group in grief. A feeling of panic can be very dangerous when it spreads from one person to the next. I am learning to be alert when I have a change from my usual mood. I try to find the cause of the new spirit in me. If I absorb any spirit that conflicts with God's spirit, I can choose to reject it. Daily I hear about violence. Music and entertainment describe infidelity. Ads urge me to be self-indulgent. Just living a normal life will expose me to thoughts that pull my awareness away from oneness with God. Because each day's events push me a little bit away from God, it is necessary to set time each day to move back toward God. Each evening I consciously remove from myself any negative spirit that has gotten a foothold in me during the day. I state once again my choice to be filled with the spirit of God. Every time I wake up (even from a nap) I renew my connection with God by thinking these things:

God made me and gives me life.
God's spirit is in every cell in my body.
God's light surrounds me and protects me.
Dear God, let your light shine clearly in me.
Let your light shine through me to everyone I meet.
Let me be a channel of your blessings to others.

My evening prayer is:

Infinite and loving God,
    pour your spirit through me.
Wash from me all that conflicts with your spirit.
Fill me with your holy spirit, your light;
    let me be clean.
Your light shines in me and heals me.
Your light surrounds me and protects me.
I am protected by the power of your name.

I was taught as a child that it is good to say prayers before bed. I find the effects of pre-sleep prayer so good that I now end each day that way.

In recent years I have become more psychically sensitive, so I am sometimes aware of the presence of some types of negative spirits. The Bible calls these negative energies "unclean spirits". Jesus was effective at removing unclean spirits from people when he spoke that intention. We can also dismiss a spirit "in the name of Jesus Christ". This works even when done by people who are not Christians. The Bible reports that some who did not follow Jesus successfully cast out spirits in his name even before he died.[28] I notice that on the days I have used my morning and evening prayers I do not sense negativity around me or feel any unexplained uneasiness.

*

Besides keeping my body spiritually cleaned up, I like to ask for God's light to also fill my home. I pray that my home will be so filled with God's light that everyone who enters may feel God's presence. I have lived in a number of different houses in the past twenty-five years. No matter where I live people have mentioned a nice feeling they sense in my home. Interestingly, these comments are usually said as people walk near the place where I sit to pray, though they don't realize it. Whatever we dedicate to God's use becomes special. And many people are sensitive enough to sense it. What a delightful place the world would be if everything in it was dedicated to God's use!

There have been some times that I have felt a need to cleanse a house in a spiritual way. The first time came while I was painting walls inside a farmhouse that had been vacant for twenty years. I worked in the house with several other people for a few days. Then I was left to work by myself for a few hours. As I quietly worked, I began to feel uneasy. I reminded myself that it was a very safe community and that helpful neighbors lived nearby. I took my paintbrush and painted a cross over the door of the room. That made me feel more at ease. It was an odd thing for me to do, though, because I have never lived in a home where crosses were displayed in that way. I painted the walls a little longer and then painted a cross over each window. When I found myself tempted to paint a cross above a mouse hole so that every opening into the room would be covered, I put down my paintbrush. It was time to face the fact that there was a feeling in the house that I didn't like.

I sat down and began to pray. I prayed that the room would be filled with God's light. As I prayed I felt a strong wave of sadness come over me. I prayed that all the sadness that had filled the house be washed out the windows by God's light. I prayed like this for more than half an hour, until the sense of sadness was gone. Then I imagined the house filled with a beautiful bright light. I asked God to fill every corner and crack with light. After that the house felt fine to me, even when I was alone. Later I learned that the last occupant of the house had hung himself there. Neighbors thought the house was haunted, which explains why it was vacant so long. I have done "spiritual house cleaning" several other times. This is how I cleaned our own house after my daughter saw the ghost there.

Light is more powerful than darkness. I believe that this is one of the most important teachings of the Bible. Jesus pointed out that if you put a light in a dark room, the light causes darkness to disappear. It is *always* this way. Light can overcome darkness, but darkness has no power to put out a light. I taught this to my children when they were very young, and I wish I could teach it to every person in the world. It is important to always remember this truth. I will say it again: Light is *more* powerful than darkness.

*

I have talked, so far, about removing obstructions that make it difficult to bring spirit into our lives. There are other things we can do to increase our ability to combine spirit and matter. There are exercises that will strengthen our awareness or willpower for this work. People who do physical exercise every day become stronger. This is also true spiritually. Just as there are many activities that can strengthen arm muscles, there are a number of ways to strengthen control of the will.

Many religions have practices that must be done repeatedly. A lot of people pray or meditate every day. Monks and devout Muslims (and others) have many prayer times each day. Specific words must be prayed at specific times. Why? Surely God is *always* listening, not just at those times of day. The purpose is to make the person who prays stronger. It is hard to do anything repeatedly, no matter how simple the task. It is easy to miss prayer times because of forgetting, being overworked, or being absorbed in other interests. Excuses often cover up laziness. A task that is repetitive uncovers our priorities. How important is God to me? It may not matter very much which spiritual task I do repeatedly. They will all test my promise to put God first in my life. They strengthen will. Willpower is a wonderful thing when it is used to serve God.

When I do a practice like this, I am using part of my day to do an activity that demonstrates that God is in charge of my life. I have never had five prayer times a day. People who do this need to keep God in mind throughout the day, in order not to miss a prayer time. (This benefit is lessened if an alarm is used as a reminder.) To remember each prayer time requires constant alertness to the duty that is to be done for God. Meditating daily is a similar discipline.

Another way to strengthen control of the will is to repeat some very ordinary activity every day. I heard of someone who moved a pencil from one side of the room to the other every morning. In the evening he would move it back to where it had been. The following day would be the same. It seems like a useless thing to do. But it isn't useless because it strengthens the will. That is the very purpose of it. Excuses rise up: "I'm too busy" "I'm tired" "This is a silly thing to do" "I'll do it later" "I probably don't need to do it *every* day." A discipline begins to change me when I break through this resistance and do it anyway.

It is not the particular action of the discipline that changes me. It is the *struggle* to do the discipline that makes me grow. Whatever discipline I choose, doing it repeatedly will gradually give me stronger control of my will. It takes control of will to put God in charge. I am inspired by the words of Joshua, "As for me and my household, we will serve God"; Mary, "Let it be done in me according to your word"; and Jesus, "Not my will, Father, but let your will be done." These words show great self-control and inner strength. Willpower is essential to spiritual growth. It should not be thrown out or given away. Great steps in spirituality were not made by people with weak wills. The key is to gain control of one's own will.

*

Will provides the power to take action, but it does not decide what the action will be. Actions are formed by desires. I have instinctual desires, of course, like survival. I desire to stay alive and to support myself. But *how* I do these things reflects other desires. I desire to live harmoniously with other people and with nature; I desire to be helpful; I desire to be healthy, and so forth. Even though I don't think about these values all the time, they influence the choices I make.

In order for my day-to-day activities to be spiritual, I need to be holding a desire that patterns my activities in that way. I call this desire my spiritual ideal. It guides the choices I make. Because of this, the spiritual ideal I hold causes or influences many of my experiences. I have used several different spiritual ideals in my life, and I find they have affected how my life developed. Making a clear choice about what spiritual ideal to hold is very likely the most important single step a person can take for spiritual growth. I was lucky when a spiritual ideal, "I want to be one with God!" bubbled up inside me. Usually people need to do a lot more work than that to arrive at a spiritual ideal.

One way to find an ideal is to make a list of the people you most admire, and the qualities you admire them for. A number of the qualities in the list might be suitable for use as a spiritual ideal. I believe the ultimate ideal is the Christ pattern: the full interpenetration of body and spirit. But that is too much to start with; it takes a lot of strength and control and balance to hold the Christ pattern as the ideal. Unless you are ready to give your life for others, it may be best to begin with one of the components of this highest ideal, such as kindness, understanding or forgiveness.

After a few years with one of these, a different one could be tried. The strengths and learning you gain from using one ideal will deepen your work with the next ideal. It may not matter too much where you begin, other than to begin where you are. Eventually your spiritual path will lead you into every aspect of life. There is no part of our lives that does not have a relationship to God.

*

Suppose I have chosen the ideal of forgiveness…I need to look through all of my relationships, past and present, to see if I hold any resentments or grudges. If I find any, and I surely will, I need to let them go. I need to release the resentments and grudges from my heart, mind, and memory, and never return to them. This does not mean that the things I had resented have ceased to be bad if they, in fact, were. It means that I have removed myself from being the cosmic judge of these acts. That is God's job, not mine. God is very capable of remembering and dealing with a bad deed done to me or anyone else. We often forget this. We wish God would judge and punish during the course of *this* life, which is how *we* would have to do it if we were in charge. But when I hold the ideal of forgiveness, I pause and reflect and realize that I never really was elected to be Judge of the Cosmos. When I have the humility to step out of that role, I move into a healthier relationship with God, as well as with other people. Having done that, I might think I have won my Achievement Award in Forgiveness and I am now ready to move on to a new ideal.

But let's not be so quick to leave this issue. I continue to keep forgiveness as my spiritual ideal so that it becomes part of my routine way of looking at the world. Before many months have passed I notice the old judgmental feelings coming up in me when I listen to the news. My heart fills with resentment toward people who, through their own selfishness, have harmed other people. Jesus taught his followers to forgive people who are so sorry for what they have done that they will never do it again. Jesus could forgive even the people who killed him, but he *did* throw some people out of the temple. Keeping a forgiving spirit while working to protect the innocent is a real challenge!

I continue working with my ideal a few more months. Then I realize that there are things *I* have done and said that I have never forgiven *myself* for. Is it even harder for me to forgive myself than for me to forgive others? If I am truly sorry for what I have done, God forgives me. If God forgives me but I don't forgive myself, does this mean I think I am smarter than God? That's a spiritual problem. I will need to find an ideal that can help me remember that I am not more important than God.

It is best to work with an ideal for a period of time, in order for it to work its maximum benefit. Each time I recognize a problem and begin to wrestle with it, I develop new strength and awareness. This, in turn, gives me a new way to look at things, so I can see more than I did before. Over time, I go more deeply into the issue. The ideal scans through the secrets in my heart, turning up attitudes I hold that do not match the ideal. I may not be able to let go of an attitude, but even to admit that it is present in me causes me to grow. The more deeply I go, the more I gain in self-understanding. I become aware of attitudes that reduce my connectedness to God, and then I can work to clear away these obstructions. As I use an ideal that represents a quality I see in God, my life moves more into conformity with that quality. For me, working with ideals has been a primary pathway to connection with God.

*

Bringing my attitudes into greater conformity with God is a huge step in spiritual growth. But it does not interpenetrate spirit and matter. There need to be actions that flow from the attitudes. We need to make our spiritual intentions concrete in actual words and deeds. There are a number of ways to do this. Jesus said to his closest followers, "If you love me, feed my sheep" which was a poetic way of telling them to take care of other people as an expression of their love for him.

We can do acts of kindness as an expression of respect for the divine in other people. People in many faiths have realized that they feel closer to God when they do good things for people who are not in a position to return the favor. Religious people have been active for centuries giving free food to hungry people, sending clothing to victims of disasters, and caring for the sick. Individuals can express their love of God by finding opportunities to do good deeds like visiting a lonely person. There are so many lonely people who ache for someone to speak to: an elderly person living alone, someone having a long stay at the hospital or someone who has recently moved to the area.

A spiritual discipline is another way to make concrete expression of a person's relationship with God. My first spiritual discipline was a bedtime prayer. When I was very small my mother said a prayer aloud as I lay in my bed. For the first years the prayer was, "Thank you, Father, for this day and for all of its blessings." Later she added, "Please help Janet and Punkin' to get well," which referred to children I knew, a girl with cerebral palsy and a boy with hemophilia. After a few years my mother told me each night to think the prayer silently on my own, and to let her know when I was finished. This established a pattern of thinking about God on schedule, once a day. I fell away from the practice at some point during my teen years, but nevertheless, I had had the experience of following a regular spiritual discipline. Because of this I have never doubted that I could do a spiritual discipline if I decided to.

People all over the world have spiritual disciplines. There are more types of disciplines than you can imagine. Some people make up private disciplines that they never mention to anyone else. Other people take on public disciplines that show to the world that they follow a certain religion. Just about everyone wears clothing, but some people select what they wear to show their relationship to God. Some women never wear pants and other women always do. Some men cover their heads to pray; other men uncover their heads. While these disciplines appear to be opposites, they have the same purpose. All of these people by following their clothing disciplines show to themselves, to their religious community, and to the public that God is in charge of their lives. Following a spiritual discipline intermixes spiritual beliefs with physical reality. There are times when it is inconvenient or embarrassing to follow a discipline, even a simple one like saying a prayer of thanks before a meal. I seem to get more inner growth than usual when I carry out my spiritual intentions under difficult conditions. My guess is that the *effort* I expend on God's behalf may matter far more than the description of the activity itself.

There is something very holy about doing things for God. When we do a deed on God's behalf, our will is united with God. The deed itself is like one of God's children...a little concrete manifestation of Spirit. Each time we do a deed for God we are "birthing" it, like a "child" of God, into the earth. We receive God's life force each day. If we are willing, as Mary was, we can bring this spirit of God into manifestation.

My goal is to live in such a way that my life embodies and expresses God's spirit. Every step I make in that direction is a success. Each step I take seems so small, yet a big pile of small successes is still a big pile. I show love of God's spirit when I am kind to all people, including myself, for we carry God's love and imprint in us. I show love and respect for my body when I make an effort to nurture it properly with healthy foods and enough exercise and rest. I show my love and appreciation to God by setting aside some of my time each day to be aware of God's presence in my life. I give God a gift each time I carry out a daily activity aware of how it fits into God's use of my life.

These don't look like grand, heroic deeds. They appear too simple to bring about the cosmic event of interpenetrating God's spirit into a human life. But they only seem easy until you try them. Nothing is tested until it is put to use. It is easier to talk about spirituality than to live it. And God seems to notice the difference. Over and over I have noticed that when I put a spiritual concept into action, God responds in some way. This is the musicless dance.

# Chapter Seven: **BALANCE**

When I am using all my daily energy for God's purposes, I feel that I have come home. I feel comfortable within myself. I feel whole. If only I could stay in this pattern of living always! My feelings are like those expressed by David thousands of years ago, "God's goodness and mercy will be with me for the rest of my life, and I will live in the house of God forever." Why go anywhere when what you want is where you are? You would think I'd stay there, but I don't.

There is something in me that says, "If *some* is good, then *more* is better! Surely if spirit in my life is good, then the more spirit the better." Many of us learn the hard way that it is possible to have too much of a good thing. Food is good but I have learned that it is possible to eat so much that my stomach hurts. What about spirituality? Can I overdose on prayer? Maybe. It is a question of balance.

Body and spirit are both expressions of God. I must bring them together for God's light to be visible through my actions. Even though each is good, it is possible to have too much of a good thing. A woman (or man) can focus too much on the material world or on herself. If she does, she may believe that she is better than everybody else. She might ignore the views of others, believe that goodness is based on wealth, or seek satisfaction through self-indulgence. On the other hand, it is also possible to lean too far in the opposite direction. If she thinks that the material world is fundamentally bad, she may try to escape into spirituality. Having a sense of the worthlessness about her own life, she might think of herself as a doormat to be walked over by others. She might lack initiative or willingness to stand up for her beliefs. She could forget to provide for her own needs and those of her family. She might dislike her own body and welcome physical suffering.

People are complex and can hold more than one value system. That makes it possible to alternate between doing too much and too little of something. I have at least dabbled in the problems on both lists. In varying situations I have had either too high or too low an opinion of myself. In some situations I am reluctant to say what I think; at other times I fail to listen or I insist I am right. I have certainly indulged in eating more food than I needed to.

Of all the examples mentioned, I think the expectation of suffering has had the biggest impact on my life. Even my first ideal, "…to be one with God," became skewed by negative beliefs I had about myself. I thought that in order to be spiritual I needed to somehow erase myself. To do this, I often suppressed my feelings. Even though I gained in spiritual awareness by using an ideal, I simultaneously developed hypersensitivities and other health problems. Now I try hard to discover and root out attitudes I hold that invite illness or difficult situations.

I was wrong to think God wants me to suffer. Actually God wants me to have a loving heart, not a destroyed body. One day I was startled to realize that there is no evidence Jesus had health problems, even though he demonstrated the ultimate in spiritual connectedness. This convinced me that it must be possible to have a healthy spirit and healthy body at the same time. I decided to claim the healthiness I saw in Jesus. I changed my expectations about my body. I then prayed for God to make my body match my new expectations of healthiness. My health made a sudden turn toward normality and the process moved swiftly.

For the most part, the negative attitudes I have held were not taught to me. I chose them in the process of developing my relationship with God. I had good intentions when I made the choices. I chose them because I thought they would bring me spiritual growth. Even though my motives were good, these attitudes still damaged my health. Choice is so important. God gives each of us the right to make our own choices. This ability to choose is at the very core of what it is to be human. The choices we make determine the course of our lives. Life is a period of time during which we make choices and harvest the results of those choices.

Even though I chose some bad attitudes, God did not overrule my choices. God gave an instant response to prayers about my broken arm. But when I prayed about allergies God seemed to be deaf. I believe that prayer does not heal things we have chosen for ourselves, even if we have forgotten that we chose them.[29] Perhaps because God does not interfere in choices, illnesses that come directly from choices are outside God's area of activity. Having reached this way of thinking, I tried praying for God to throw out all the wrong choices I had made. I'm sorry to report that the attempt failed. In my experience, God has not eliminated my negative attitudes in response to generalized prayers. It has been necessary that I first recognize what negative attitude I am holding. If I name the attitude and ask God to remove it, it is done.

I remember a time when I prayed to have a specific negative attitude removed from me. The attitude was the desire to be thought well of by other people. I would worry if other people misunderstood me or looked down on me. It is not an uncommon attitude. But it is contrary to the teachings of Jesus, and it causes a lot of anxiety. I had tried for a number of years to free myself from it, but failed. It was ingrained in me and was stubbornly persistent. So I prayed for help removing the attitude. A week later I realized that I had not had that attitude for the entire week. The week has now become years, and I rarely see evidence of that attitude. I am delighted.

I alternate between rigidity (an overdose of materiality) and a lack of boundary (an excess of spirit). Running back and forth between two extremes is not balance. I need to learn how to stand in the middle in a balanced way. I need to learn to integrate spirit and matter in my daily life. This is the task of my spiritual journey. Here is a picture that helps me: If I want to travel to a city that is 200 miles away, I need to prepare in two ways. First I have to figure out what route to take to get there. That is the "spirit" of the trip. Second, I have to put fuel in the tank. That is the physical part. I won't get where I want to go unless I do. To make the trip, I need to know where I'm going and I need the material means to get there.

*

Keeping spirit and matter balanced is not my only problem. Sometimes I use spirit and matter backwards in my life. This is a bit like trying to use the destination of the trip as fuel. I don't always remember to use physical realities to meet physical needs, and spiritual realities for spiritual needs. But it is surprisingly easy to mix them up. Our culture has things so turned around that it is easy to get confused. Sometimes children learn to love things and use people instead of learning how to love people and use things. *Things* are part of the material world, but they sometimes drift into spiritual life, as a way to measure how good someone is. Goodness has to do with a person's ideals and ways of treating other people. These are spiritual qualities. Money and the things we own are physical. If we think rich people are better than those who don't have any money, that idea will cut down our connection with God.

We don't need to abandon the material world. We just need to learn how to use it correctly. Money can be used in good ways or bad ways, and that can be said of almost anything in the material world. We need to be careful that we do not use money or the things we can buy as a way to measure our lives. Our ideals and what we worship measure our lives. It is best to keep our ideals, the control tower that guides our lives, from getting cluttered up with material objects. But it is so difficult to truly let go of thinking about people in terms of how much money they have. I have always had some friends who were wealthy and others who had very little after paying for rent, food and heat. I have been unsuccessful at bringing all these people together at parties. Rich people are uncomfortable in a social setting with poor people. I find poor people even more uncomfortable around rich people. Throughout history people have stratified their societies on the basis of what is owned. Jesus turned that idea upside down, which I am sure was shocking at the time. Now, two thousand years later, it seems to be just as shocking. It's not that money is bad. It's just that we need to get it out of our values, out of our ideals. I think this value system problem is what Jesus was talking about when he said that we couldn't worship both God and money. We need to learn to *use* money...use it in ways that agree with our spiritual values.

It takes daily effort to keep spirit and matter in the right places. They are both good, but they are both different. And soul is involved with each one. That's one reason why the spiritual path gets tricky. It would be much simpler if our souls were only involved in "spiritual things" and kept out of "real life". But that's not how we were made. The soul functions both in spirit and matter.

*

Some people can feel the soul's activity in various parts of the body. Some know what a "pure heart" feels like. We are certain that "inspiration" happens in the head. We feel it there. Remember the chakras? These are locations where many religions have noticed a bodily response to spirit. The "heart" is pointed to by each of the major religions. People from a variety of religious backgrounds find the soul active in a series of locations, from the base of the spine to the top of the head. The contact points in the head are where spirit enters our consciousness. These are the chakras that have to do with inspiration, visions and spiritual healing. The lower chakras do a lot to bring spirit together with the physical body. The gonads are always included as one of the contact points where spirit and matter meet.

It startles us to think of the soul having anything to do with sex, but the Bible describes the union between God and the chosen people in sexual terms. Sometimes when Israel is unfaithful to God the nation is described as God's unfaithful wife who is having sex with other gods. The similarity between the electric quality of both orgasm and healing prayer reminds me that the soul interfaces both with the gonads and the pituitary. I think many of us would behave better if we felt that our sexual activities were being done with our souls!

Imagine the soul moving its awareness back and forth between the pineal/pituitary (divine guidance/spiritual healing) and the gonads (physical creation).[30] When I try to picture this, I think of a long cylindrical area with a magnetic field at each end. Perhaps I get this idea from the vision I had when I was a teenager. I think of my soul as having consciousness that can move its awareness back and forth between awareness of myself as an individual and awareness of being a part of all creation (awareness of being God-stuff). When I am deep in meditation I may become so absorbed in awareness of oneness with God that I lose awareness of my individuality. But a moment later an itch on my nose could bring my awareness back down to my body and to myself as an individual. I think the soul has these two poles of activity because it is the point of contact between spirit and matter. Soul is the interface of spirit and matter.

*

My soul, which is the essence of who I am, functions at both of these levels. I am one with all that is, but I am also a unique individual. It is helpful not to get these levels mixed up. If I receive inspiration, my awareness is at the level of spirit. But if I think, "Because I received the inspiration, I am really great," then my awareness has plunged from the oneness to my particu-

## DANCE OF THE SOUL

Body and spirit meet in us. We have been designed to be open both to the physical world of our bodies and to the non-physical world of spirit. We can only pay full attention to one at a time so we alternate between the two.

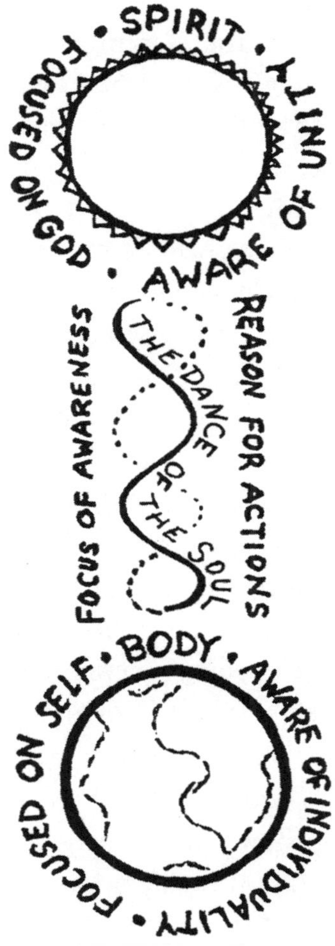


If we pay attention to only one of these, we can do little to bring spirit into the world.

lar individuality. I am confused if I think what is universal belongs to me in particular. It is *very* important to never take personal credit for inspiration that comes from God. If I do, I am denying God's action and I am putting myself in God's place. These are big problems for me, spiritually.

It is also important not to take credit for spiritual healing. If I take credit after a spiritual healing has taken place, I am claiming to my own credit what is rightfully God's. If I claim to be the source of healing before the healing takes place, a different problem can come up. Thought directs spirit. If I claim to be the source of healing, then it very likely will be my own personal energy that goes to the other person. That person may indeed get well if I heal in this way. But the problem is that in this way of healing, the healer can take on the illness. A person who channels God's healing energy will feel more energized after a healing session. If my energy feels depleted after praying for someone, then I try to figure what went wrong.

I now pay attention any time I feel my energy becoming depleted. I had a friend who called on the phone several times a week (and sometimes daily) over the course of many years. She talked about her struggles with daily life. Her difficulties were great and she was dear to me, so I felt sympathetic. She would usually talk more than half an hour, often an hour. I always felt tired out after the calls. I finally began to wonder if the tiredness I felt meant I was, without realizing it, healing with personal energy. The next time she called I made the silent prayer, "O.K., God, This one is on you, not me..." Within a couple of minutes my friend was asking how my family and I were doing. That startled me because in all her other calls, she had only focused on her own difficulties. After about ten minutes, she had received all the "help" she needed and hung up...the shortest call ever! And I felt energized, not depleted. So I realized that I had indeed been giving little healings all those years. But what I gave was never enough. God does the job right! I had been bringing the tiredness onto myself by thinking of *myself* as the source of help for my friend.

One time I prayed at the hospital for a friend with two broken legs. Though I didn't realize it, he thought of me as the source of healing. Perhaps he flattered me with his thanks, or I was too pleased with myself. By the time I got home I had pains in both of my legs at the sites of his bone breaks. Realizing what was going on, I called him up and asked him to expect healing from God and not from me. I am willing to help, but not with my body's personal energy! The pains went away promptly. I am willing to be a *channel* of healing, but *not a source* of it. God is the source. I am an expression of God, I am a part of God, but I am not God, the infinite source. I am an individual part of the Oneness. But I can't confuse my individuality with my existence in the Oneness.

If I feel proud of myself for being "spiritual" I get into big trouble. Within a day I begin having a sense of becoming separated from God. I do not like it at all; it frightens me. Jesus had to deal with the temptations of Satan immediately after the voice of God said he was the Son of God and that God was pleased with him. Maybe this tempted him to be proud of his spirituality. But he didn't fall into that trap. Spiritual pride is a big problem. We might fantasize that we, with all our limitations, are the source of our own goodness. That is more than just an over-inflated view of self. It is like claiming equality with God, which suggests that God is no greater than a human who doesn't even know how to digest his meals or make his own blood circulate!

When a person thinks he is the greatest, it means that he is only looking at himself. He has cut off his awareness of connection with God. So it is possible to use spirituality in such a way that it moves us away from God. Excessive self-admiration, even on account of spiritual growth, distances a person from God. It is simply because attention is focused more on self and less on God. But regardless of the reason, it is scary to be separated in awareness from God. I feel a lot closer to God when I am able to avoid feeling self-important.

Since connection to God is the goal of spiritual efforts, I am interested in anything I can do that helps. I have found that developing an attitude of humility has been very helpful. We were all created "good", but none of us is "the greatest". I try to remember that I am part of a large group (humanity). God has created many of us and each one of us has God's imprint. I try to remember that concept because, when I do, it helps keep my consciousness closer to the Oneness.

*

Having noticed how helpful humility is for my spiritual life, I experimented with trying to hold onto that attitude for an entire day. I was surprised to find it so hard. For me the difficulty came in trying to think of myself as being no better or more important than any other person. Up until then I thought I had spent my life believing in equality. I discovered the shallowness of my belief as soon as I took on "humility" as a spiritual discipline. I watched my attitudes toward the various people I saw walking through town or shopping in stores. To my surprise I found that I was judging each one. As soon as I saw someone my mind would sort and classify the person by their sex, race, weight, height, attractiveness, and clothing quality. I could not prevent my mind from making comparisons, such as "I am better looking than he is" or "She probably has more money than I do." These constant thoughts racing through me like a babbling brook were not expressions of humility.

Unable to stop myself from the hundreds of little judgments I was making each day, I settled for mentally apologizing each time I passed judgment. After two days, I was getting quite good at this. I knew it was making me a better person, so I felt proud of myself. I felt proud. The moment I had some success in becoming more humble, the success itself made me less humble. Because I was less humble and had focused my thoughts on myself, my consciouseness moved away from God.

How ironic it was that success in humility would

make me less humble and move me farther from God! I became frustrated and exasperated. " I don't think it is *humanly* possible to be humble," I mentally shouted to God in prayer. Instantly I realized the deeper truth of my statement. As long as *I* am the one who is making me humble, I will never be able to be truly humble. "O.K.," I said to God, "*You* do it!" As soon as I said that, I felt deep peace and humility. I knew that God had accomplished it for me and I did not deserve the credit for it. I felt thankful to the point of tears. This experience gave me personal understanding that full reconnection with God is a gift from God. It is not something we can do for ourselves.

We are children of God and God carries us. In the animal world we see two very different ways that babies travel with their parents. The cat family carries its young by the scruff of the neck, with the kitten dangling helplessly. Monkey parents do not hold onto their little ones as they swing through the trees with them. Instead, the baby clings onto its parent. In the connection between people and God, both methods are used. We use our efforts to hold on...*and* God carries us. I think both methods are necessary in order for a person to reconnect with God. If a person does not want to be connected with God, it won't happen. But a person who desires to connect with God can't do it without God's help. It is a bit like marriage between two people: a marriage happens only if *both* want it to happen. It does not happen if only one person wants to get married. Interestingly, some people who became reconnected with God called their experience a mystical marriage.

*

Most of us are not that far along. More likely we are having an occasional "date" with God...or perhaps we are still trying to figure out how to start a conversation. Fortunately we are not all alone on our personal spiritual journey. There are many people who have been on this same road before us who are happy to give advice and encouragement. It is important for me to remember that my spiritual journey does not begin and end with me. It is more than a matter of just me interacting with God. Spiritually we are team players. Before I started in this direction I had *heard* that God existed. I had been *shown* how to help other people. There are many people who, in different ways, *encouraged* me toward being good. I find it is very useful each day to remind myself about these people and to remember that I am not journeying alone.

I thank God for many of the people whose efforts have helped me in my journey. Often I start with appreciation for the faith tradition that led me to God. I thank God for Abraham, Moses, and some of my favorite prophets. I wouldn't have heard of their experiences with God except that there were generations of people who memorized the stories and passed them on to their children. I thank God for Jesus and his family and friends. I appreciate all the people who had a hand in getting his story to me. Some of these people lost their lives for passing the information along. Every day I try to remember as many as I can of the people who have helped me become more connected to God. I name each person. Some are friends, teachers and pastors. Some are people who have inspired me when I read about them, like Albert Schweitzer, Mother Teresa of Calcutta, and St. Teresa of Avila. The list always includes my parents, who lived their faith even when it was personally costly.

One person who inspired me when I was a child was Jeannette Holmes, whose grandmother has been a slave. Jeannette's trust in God deeply impressed me. At age six, she was alone outdoors when her dress suddenly burst into flames. (Something burning had been tossed from an upper window.) There was no one there to help her. Jeannette was terrified and was about to run. But she remembered that her uncle had said, "When you are in trouble, get on your knees and pray to Jesus." She fell to her knees, put her face in her hands and began to scream to Jesus to help her. A neighbor heard her screams, though he couldn't see her because of a fence. He jumped the fence and threw his coat on her to smother the fire. If Jeannette had run, the wind would have made the fire worse, and she would probably have died. She always had scars on her back and arms, but there were no burns on her face because she had put her face in her hands to pray.

When I knew her, Jeannette's main pleasure was singing hymns, and we sang hymns together. Her biggest regret about progressive blindness was that she could no longer read the Bible. Leaving the future in God's hands, she would say, "I'll see you next week, if it is the Lord's will." Materially Jeannette Holmes had very little, but spiritually she had a lot. I was blessed that she shared what she had with me.

The list of people who have helped me goes on and on. I express my appreciation for those who have loved and supported me. My husband is always in this list, along with some relatives, in-laws, and very special friends. My children and grandchildren are a joy. I have always thanked God for them. Every day I try to add someone new, someone I never thanked God for. Sometimes I thank God for the people who inspired and taught the people who, in turn, have inspired and taught me. It is really pleasant to spend some time each day remembering people who have made my life better.

On the days that I have remembered to give thanks for people who have helped me in my spiritual journey I feel far more connected spiritually. I do not pray to those people; I thank God for them. But when I do, I feel connected to a huge pool of spirituality and I have a sense of being part of a community. On those days I use this prayer I have a deepened feeling of safety and peace. I have learned to love the effects of this prayer and I try hard not to have a day slip by without my prayer of thanks.

*

It is very important for me to think inclusively, even globally, and in terms of community when spirit is the focus of my awareness. Especially when I am consciously aware of the flow of God's energy, I need to avoid thinking about myself. These include the times I am involved in healing prayer, visions or meditation or when I am being inspired.

At other times I do need to look at myself - to consider my motivations, and to compare my actions to my ideals. It seems strange that it can be "spiritual" to think about myself, and it can also be "spiritual" to not think about myself. How can this be?

A lot of spiritual issues are paradoxes. (A "paradox" is when two things which seem to be opposite are both true.) Christianity is full of paradoxes, for example Jesus as both human and God, as both servant and Master, Jesus who was killed and alive again afterward. God is paradoxical, too, being infinite yet very personally within each person. Spirit has appeared as fire and as water. Spiritual experiences can feel like filling or emptying...the list goes on and on.

It helps me to understand paradoxes to think of soul (or God or Christ) as functioning in two different realms. They function both in spirit and in matter, touching both infinity and limitations. In a paradox, it may be that one of the statements is true in terms of spirit, while the other is true with respect to matter or individuality. The basic nature of the soul being paradoxical may do more than *explain* the existence of paradoxes. It may even make it *necessary* for us to experience paradox.

*

Throughout this book I have been talking about the importance of bringing together spirit and matter. And now it may seem that I am talking about keeping them

## OPPOSITES

What is considered “true” may depend on whether a person looks from a spiritual point of view or from a physical perspective.

| SPIRITUAL PERSPECTIVE | PHYSICAL PERSPECTIVE |
|---|---|
| Jesus<br>is divine<br>is described as a king and as shepherd | Jesus<br>is human<br>is described as servant and as lamb |
| We are told not to focus on ourselves, and not be self centered | “Know Thyself” is important for personal growth |
| Some people purify their consciousness because of their relationship with God | Some people purify their bodies because of their relationship with God |
| We have intuition to help us understand spiritual realities | We have reason/logic to help us understand physical realities |

Spirit and matter both are part of the oneness of God

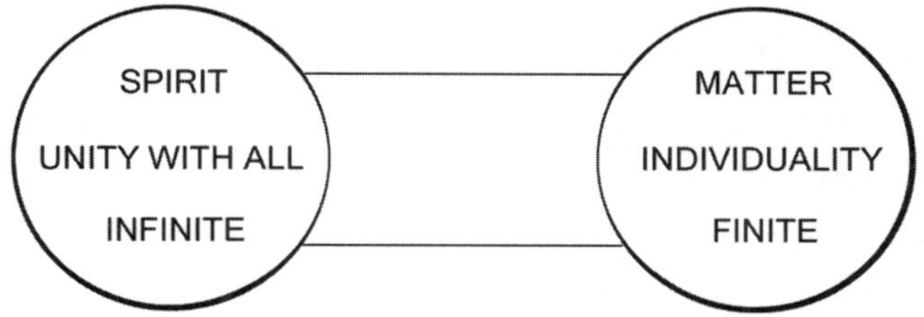

separate. But that's not the idea at all. Spirit and matter are rightfully together, and we need to learn to recognize that. Spirit and matter are joined in everything we do; they come together to produce deeds. Spirit and matter are like two people who marry. They are a single married unit, but they each continue to have their own identities.

Spirit is spirit and matter is matter even when they are joined in unity of purpose. The way in which spirit and matter are actually one is beyond comprehension (probably because of spirit being infinite). This is how I see it: Spirit and matter exist separately and as a unit in every soul. Spirit and matter exist separately and as a unit in the Oneness (God).[31] Spirit and matter exist separately and as a unit in Jesus Christ. (This is more than just *hard* to understand. We can't understand it. Our brains are not set up to take this in.)

I am fascinated by the similarity that exists in the nature of God, the nature of Jesus Christ and the nature of the soul. Each joins together Oneness and multiplicity. It's as if you could overlay their spheres of activity, one on top of each other, and they would each have the same fundamental shape at the center. They would be congruent, able to be nested in each other, like objects that all have the same shape.

Aha. My soul's activity has the same shape fundamental to all that is. Spirit and matter are different, though both are from the same source originally. Spirit and matter are both part of me; I can focus my awareness on either one. I join spirit (motivations, ideals) with my bodily forces (strength, skills, will) in every act

## CONGRUENCE: SIMILARITY OF PATTERN

God, Jesus Christ, and the human soul have in common that they are active in spirit and in matter. There are substantial differences among them. God's nature is infinite; the human soul is finite. Both of these natures are united in Christ (fully interpenetrated spirit and matter). By participating in this united nature, the individual has enhanced access to the infinite.

Some quotes by Jesus:

"Believe me that I am in the Father and the father is in me..."
"On that day you will know that I am in my Father, and you in me, and I in you."
"...As you, Father, are in me and I in you, may they also be in us..."

Holy Bible (NRSV) John 14:11, 14:20, 16:21

I do. Spirit remains spirit and body remains body, even though they are used to carry out a single task. Nevertheless, spirit and matter function as a unit in my soul.

*

My body cannot keep secrets from the spirit in me. Spirit and matter exchange information. The spiritual values I have eventually affect my health. The way I treat people, including myself, is part of my spiritual record. What happens in my life at one level is also remembered at the other level. This is because I only have one soul, and it is in both. It is in matter and spirit.

Our deeds are *so* important! They express how much we understand about God. I recently heard a woman talking about living a spiritual life. She said, "It's in the head, in the heart, and in the hands. If a spiritual truth is in the head, the hands will be doing it. If the hands aren't doing it, the truth probably didn't make a very deep impression in the head." Our deeds show how much we know.

When we turn the understanding we have gained into a deed, we actually experience that spiritual truth. Having a real experience of it gives us the deeper understanding that comes from living it. The more we act out a spiritual truth, the more we will come to know about it. Doing acts of kindness is a big part of the outer path to holiness (connecting with God by acts done for God). I have been talking mostly about the inner path because it is less well understood. The outer path also leads into God. I know this from experience.

In my early twenties I read theology books and wrestled with spiritual questions. I was uncertain about what I believed. I felt that I needed to make a huge jump from the things I understood to the things I wanted to believe. But I didn't know how to make that jump. I felt the frustration deep in my heart; I ached to be able to make the leap of faith. With tears in my eyes I asked God to let me know how to make the jump into faith. And I *heard* an answer to my prayers, something that has happened only a few times in my life. I heard actual words inside my head. The voice said, "Feed my sheep." I recognized this as one of the last things Jesus said to his students.[32] To my understanding, it meant, "Take care of people who need your help. Help those who are poor or badly treated." I volunteered everywhere I could: low cost housing, tutoring, traffic safety for children, an emergency hotline, and church work. After three years of this I felt it was time to have another period of religious study and thought. I remembered where I had left off, praying for a way to make the leap of faith. I realized that during the three years of volunteering, the "leap of faith" had taken place…and I hadn't noticed.

Helping other people had given me inner spiritual growth. But I have found that it works the other way too. Growing spiritually leads to helping people. It seems that service (helping people) is a natural result of being close to God, even if it is an inward path that gets you there. It would be difficult to be close to God without giving out love/kindness/charity to other people.

God constantly gives outward, like a fountain that never stops. Because God is so generous, the more our lives are filled with God's presence, the more generous we are likely to feel. The energy we receive from God we will allow to flow through us and beyond us. We can express it as acts of kindness. We may send it out in prayer. But we do not cling to the energy as if we were somehow the owners of it.

*

God's energy is very powerful. Like all other forms of energy, it must be handled properly to avoid problems. It does not work to handle God's energy with selfishness, wanting to be better than others because of it. It is a gift for us to receive and share. Whatever act we choose to do with God's energy puts our own individualized stamp on it. But we give the formed energy out, just as God gave it out to us.

The energy of God flows. It is important for the flow to continue. It is important not to stop the flow. I would not block the electricity in my house to cause a short circuit. I would not contain a stream of pure water to make it stagnant. I am reminded of the Israelites who wandered forty years without food supplies. Each day God provided a nutritious substance they could gather off the ground and eat. Every day God provided all that their bodies could use and even more. But if they gathered more than they actually used during the day, the leftovers became rotten, wormy and disgusting. Leftover energy may cause problems too. It is best not to take in more than we put out. God knows how much we need. If we use all we have been given to make the world a better place, God will give us more.

"My cup runs over..." Sometimes God fills us to overflowing. We will feel uncomfortably full if we do not send out the excess. If a person's head feels oversized or uncomfortably full during meditation, it is time to send energy out in prayer. Use God's energy to heal yourself, to heal others, to heal the earth, but keep it moving.[33] The more energy we take in, the more we need to put out. Perhaps this is the reason why Jesus, with full access to God's energy, poured this energy out to every atom in existence.

In this "Christ Event" spirit and matter interpenetrated. There is an ongoing effect; spirit and matter are on more familiar terms. Spirit has experienced matter. Every atom of matter has experienced spirit. I have been told these things; I did not experience them. I have also been told that we can experience spirit interpenetrating us by consciously taking Jesus Christ into us. I have done that with my quick, emergency prayers, and have had good results.

*

Prayer may work best in emergency situations. The intensity of desire that goes into a prayer seems to make a big difference in the outcome. In a real emergency, desire is very, very strong.

A friend told me a war experience she had when she was a teenager. After battle, the invading army retreated through her city. She and her mother hid in the remains of a bombed-out building. They could hear the voices of the soldiers, separated from them only by a wall. The women clung to each other, shaking with fright. They couldn't understand what the soldiers were saying because they spoke a different language. Then they heard the soldiers walking away. The footsteps faded in the distance. They waited a few minutes in silence and then began to whisper together. Suddenly a soldier burst in through the doorway. He had remained there on guard by himself when the other soldiers left. The women didn't realize he was behind the wall. He heard their whispers and realized they were hiding there. The soldier grabbed my friend by the wrist and began to drag her out of the hiding place. Blood was pulsing in him. She knew he intended to rape her. She was terrified and silently prayed, "CHRIST IN ME!!!" Immediately the soldier dropped her wrist. And he left them…looking as if he had received an electric shock on his hand.

*

For non-emergency situations there is another way to take Christ in. It is done by taking in physically (swallowing), a physical substance which has been filled with spirit. Jesus taught his disciples to do this using bread and wine. These substances are still used regularly in Christian churches. The prayer that invites spirit into the food and drink is more powerful than a single-person prayer such as you or I might use. All the people attending the religious gathering focus their intention on the request that God's spirit enter into the bread and wine. The foods are made sacred by God's response to the desire, belief and prayer. Using words and actions that have been used over and over again by millions of people for many centuries adds strength to the request. I feel that by doing so we are connected to the accumulated spirit of faith of the people who have done this in the past.

Olga Worrell, who facilitated my first experience in receiving spiritual healing, did a lot of scientific experiments with healing. In one experiment she sent healing prayer to a glass of water. The water was analyzed before and after the prayer. Worrell's prayers changed the chemistry (the viscosity) of the water. I think that if only one person, praying alone, can change the physical nature of a physical substance, a large number of people praying together could certainly change the spiritual nature of a physical substance.

I can sometimes feel a "tingly glow" going down my throat when I swallow bread and wine (or grape juice) that has been made sacred by God's response to belief and prayer. It is worth remembering that it is not the holiness of the person(s) praying over the food that puts Christ in it. The food becomes Christ-filled because Christ's spirit was invited into it. Desire. Asking. Inviting. That is the key. Because we have choice, we connect to God if, and only if, we *want* to. It is not how good we are that matters here, but how much we desire it. We don't bring goodness into the food; the food brings goodness into us.

Swallowing Christ-filled food is a handy way to take in the awareness of oneness with God. It is certainly not the only way to do it. We cannot even imagine all the ways God can connect with people. I have mentioned only a few of the inner and outer paths that many people have found useful. These and other approaches are used and combined in unique ways by each individual. Each of us has our own journey into God. I have described the one I have been taking. I hope my experiences can be helpful to you in some way. Perhaps some of the things I have tried interest you. If so, try them yourself and see if they work.

# NOTES

1 Olga Worrell was a remarkable spiritual healer. She allowed scientists to design experiments to test the effects of her prayers on things including water and single-cell organisms. The Smithsonian Institution at one time classified her as a "national treasure".

2 *A Search for God*, copyright © 1942, 1970 by Association for Research and Enlightmenment, Inc.

3 In the Catholic tradition, meditation is called "contemplation" or "centering prayer". In Catholic literature, the word "meditation" refers to a thoughtful, reflective state.

4 Jacqueline Jefferson, unpublished papers, Copake Falls NY, 1999.

5 According to a number of religious and mystical

traditions, God's energy makes connection in other glands too. For example, the thyroid has an energy that is connected to our choices (use of will). The pituitary and pineal glands are involved in spiritual healing and mystical experiences. Research shows that prayer affects the physical body. But how can spiritual energy affect physical energy unless they meet? These special places in the body are the points of contact where the spiritual and physical interface.

6 I have learned about ideals from people who have studied the work of Edgar Cayce. From altered states of consciousness, Cayce (1877-1945) gave about 110,000 pages of information (readings) covering a wide range of subjects. The sources he tapped into varied, as did the motivations for the readings, resulting in variations in accuracy and clarity. Often readings are convoluted and confusing. And, because a topic can be mentioned in thousands of isolated sentences widely scattered through the volumes, it is necessary to study for years to grasp the Cayce perspective on the subject. In spite of these difficulties, the Cayce readings are filled with gems of spiritual insight. They provide a fresh perspective on many important spiritual issues, and because of this they can trigger creative thinking. A.R.E. Press has published books by people who have spent decades researching the Cayce readings. As examples:

*Awakening the Real You: Awareness Through Dreams and Intuition,* by Nancy C. Pohle and Ellen L. Selover, copyright © 1999:

"The Cayce readings are very clear that in order to

tune into our higher selves through our intuitive capabilities, we must keep spiritual growth as our primary focal point. Maintaining regular spiritual practices is absolutely essential to establishing and nourishing that attunement.

"In addition to focused spiritual attunement, we need to be clear about our intent and clarifying our ideals. If we allow self-glorification, control over others, or a desire to simply make life easier to become our guiding motivation, we lose our connection to our true ideal. Most often, this creates a muddying effect on our intuitive senses, causing insights to become inaccurate or unreliable. To remain true to our higher selves, the readings suggest that unconditional love and service to others should be our guiding lights."

And *The Paradox of Free Will: Balancing Personal and Higher Will,* by Mark Thurston, copyright © 1997:

"Within the deepest recesses of your soul is a Spiritual Ideal. It is a "given," an archetype of your spiritual makeup. In this sense the Spiritual Ideal is the same for all souls; rather than being something you have chosen or created, it has been placed within you by the forces of Creation.

"The phrase used in the Cayce readings for this Spiritual Ideal is the universal Christ Consciousness. Take note of the use of the word "consciousness" here. An ideal…is actually a state of consciousness. Since consciousness is created by the interplay of mind and will, there is both a pattern quality (i.e., mind) and an *actualizing impetus* (i.e., will) to any ideal."

[7] The ways we use God's energy is frequently pointed out in dreams with a particular group of symbols. These archetypal symbols were the subject of much study by Carl Jung. Our protective, adrenal energy may show up in a dream in the form of a cat (any size cat, including lions and tigers). Loving energy often is represented by a bird. A man I know had a dream with both of these symbols. He dreamed that he had thoughtlessly knocked over his girlfriend's birdcage. As a result his cat killed her bird. Interpreting his dream, he realized that a recent thoughtless way he had expressed anger (cat) was damaging her loving feelings (bird). This interpretation of a dream is not automatic. Cats could represent another adrenal expression, including fear. But the dreamer knew what had been happening in his own life. He considered the possible interpretations and realized which one exactly fit his situation. I have found my own dreams very helpful as I have tried to bring my life into harmony with God. They were used a lot in the Bible as a way to receive guidance from God. For example see Job 33:14-18 and many examples of dreams including those of Joseph which prevented the death of God's Chosen People by starvation, and those which prevented Herod from killing the infant Jesus.

[8] Extensive studies by Mircea Eliade indicate that in a wide range of religions, meeting what is sacred is *the* most fundamental religious pattern.

[9] Although the Cayce readings are on disk, it is hard to locate all references to a topic because a variety of key-

words can be used, e.g. God, Creator, Creative Forces, the Father, Maker. And there are no keywords that will locate sentences in which the keyword is missing but implied.

[10] Fred Paddock, *Lectures on Psalms*, at St. Bridget's Catholic Church, Copake Falls NY, 1999.

[11] *Holy Bible* (New International Version) Genesis 6:6

[12] Oneness: both in the sense of a collection, and also as something cohesive, like a living being. To make a human analogy I could say we are like cells in the "body" of God.

[13] This concept is mentioned many times in the readings of Edgar Cayce.

[14] There are many different words that have been used to describe the essence of a person, such as Self, true self, higher self, ego, higher ego, soul, inner being, spirit, consciousness, and inner spark. Each word in the list has a variety of definitions, depending on whom you ask. In the Bible this inner self is sometimes referred to as a person's *heart* or even bowels.

[15] This, I think is what Paul Tillich meant by "religion of the concrete spirit" which he mentioned in his final book: *Christianity and the Encounter of World Religions*, Fortress Press, copyright © 1994. Tillich stated that "the inner aim of the history of religions is to become a

religion of the concrete spirit." p. 72.

[16] This foundational theme, the interpenetration of spirit and matter, is explored in theological detail by Ewert Cousins in his books *Bonaventure and the Coincidence of Opposites* and *Christ of the Twenty-first Century.*

[17] *The Outer Limits of Edgar Cayce's Power* by his sons H.L. Cayce and E.E. Cayce is an interesting study of this problem.

[18] The breadth of the meaning of Torah is discussed in the following selection from: *Judaism and Anthroposophy*, Edited by Fred Paddock and Mado Spiegler, copyright © 2003 by the Anthroposophical Society in America, Published by SteinerBooks. Pages 173-174.

> "Torah, from the King James Version of the Bible on, has usually been translated as *Law,* though a more accurate translation would be *instruction.* But even here one is likely to understand it too narrowly. Torah has many levels of meaning. It can refer to the first five books of the Bible. It can refer in an expanded sense to the Hebrew Bible as a whole. But it can also refer to more than one text or book: it can refer to 'the entire revelation and the entire activity of Jewish study throughout the generations ...(in fact) it can be said that all Jewish study is Torah and all Torah has the validity of revelation. Its authority rests with God, but

its agents are human beings. Throughout time Jews have always seen their primary occupation as being part of this devotion to study, this ongoing revelation.' (Barry Holtz)

"We can picture Torah as an inverted pyramid with the Bible at its base, expanded outwardly through the Mishnah, the Talmuds, the commentaries, the legal codes, the mystical tradition, the philosophical books, and the Midrashic literature. (Holtz) We are also reminded that there is a cosmological level in interpreting the concept of Torah. According to a Midrash, God looked into Torah to create the world. (Rabbi Arthur Green) In other words, God needed Torah as a blueprint in order to create the world. One can see here how the close connection between Torah and 'Wisdom' (Chokmah-Sophia) developed."

19 Fred Paddock, *Lectures on Psalms.*

20 *Holy Bible* (Revised Std Version) Isaiah 65:1-2

21 *Holy Bible* (NIV) Jeremiah. 3:19-20

22 I draw heavily upon Karl Jaspers' understanding of the evolution of consciousness, as expanded upon by Ewert Cousins in *Christ of the 21st Century*, Element

copyright © 1992, and other writings by Cousins.

23 Ewert Cousins has observed that "personal" religion appears to have arisen with the evolution of individuated consciousness.

24 *Holy Bible*, John 14:12

25 *Christianity and the Encounter of World Religions*, Paul Tillich, Fortress Press, copyright © 1994. P.72.

26 *Holy Bible*, John 5:19

27 I use "Jeshua" when speaking historically, but "Jesus" when using his name for prayer. Here I choose to use the Greek translation of his name, because it is the version that has been used for many centuries. It can be helpful to use a prayer or worship form which has facilitated interpenetration of spirit and matter in the minds and hearts of many people. Forms that have been sanctified through the worship experience of many people unites us in worship with a huge number of God-loving people throughout the centuries.

28 See *Remarkable Healings* by Shakuntala Modi, M.D, Hampton Roads Publishing Company, copyright © 1997 for further information on this topic.

29 This is my own opinion, and it is shared by Meredith Puryear, author of *Healing through Meditation and Prayer,* A.R.E. Press.

[30] This reflects my interpretation of certain of the Cayce readings on the soul.

[31] Oneness includes the uncreated infinite and every particle of matter

[32] These students (disciples) were grown men who traveled with Jesus, helping him in his work and trying to learn all that he taught.

[33] I have prayed with Jews who believed that when praying for oneself or family, selfishness is avoided by including a prayer for everyone else who has that same problem.

# BIBLIOGRAPHY

***Bonaventure and the Coincidence of Opposites*** by Ewert H. Cousins, copyright © 1978 Franciscan Herald Press. [This book deals with paradox. Theological language is used in this book. "The mystical aspects of Bonaventure's Christology are grounded in the cosmological-soteriological aspects, on the one hand, and in the notion of the soul as image of God, on the other. The soul as image is itself a form of the coincidence of opposites; for in the soul, the infinite is reflected in the finite."]

***Christ of the 21st Century,*** copyright © 1992 Ewert H. Cousins. Element. [This is also theology, but somewhat easier to read. Cousins discusses the development of human consciousness and makes a case for dialogue among world religions.]

***The Gethsemani Encounter***, Donald W. Mitchell &

James Wiseman, O.S.B., Editors. Copyright © 1999 by Monastic Interreligious Dialogue. Continuum Publishing Company (1998). [This book is a series of articles on the spiritual life by Buddhist and Christian monastics, but includes an article by Ewert Cousins, who is not a monastic. Cousin writes a short, clear statement about evolving human consciousness (primal, axial and the consciousness of today). He describes how changing consciousness has altered religion and the spiritual journey.]

***Healing Through Meditation and Prayer***, Meredith Puryear. Copyright © 1979 A.R.E. Press, reprinted 1999. [Puryear heads the Glad Helpers healing group, which has been meeting weekly for seventy years and offers laying-on-hands prayer sessions. This book describes the approach to meditation and prayer that I have used.]

***The Paradox of Free Will: Balancing Personal and Higher Will***. Copyright © 1987 Mark Thurston. A.R.E. Press, 1997. [Thurston is a psychologist. In this book he discusses will, ideals, and "finding your soul's purpose".]

## INDEX BY TOPIC

Page numbers locate discussion of the concept, but keywords may not be present in the text.

# A

# B



# C

# F



# G



(continued on next page)

# H



# I

# J



# L

(continued)

# P

# S

## Spiritual Understanding Network, LLC

The Spiritual Understanding Network encourages individuals to connect more actively with God and to share their experiences with one another. S.U.N. is neither a membership organization nor a religious group. It is a corporation engaged in publishing and advocating for spiritual life.

The Spiritual Understanding Network focuses on behaviors, attitudes, and activities that have been widely reported to effect connection with God. S.U.N. hopes to contribute to continuing public and academic discussion of these topics through future publications and conferences. We aim to wed academic precision with the language of the public.

Human experience of the divine is the starting point of religion. Interacting with God continues to be an option available to people willing to explore it. S.U.N. encourages individuals to cultivate a direct personal relationship with God. For centuries people have responded to an inner urge to connect with God. A variety of approaches and preparations have been used. Contemporary seekers may find it useful to learn from the experiences of others, past and present, who have traveled this road. S.U.N. encourages individuals to share their personal experiences of God with one another. Although each person needs only one path to God, it can be exciting to share with people who have had different experiences. Sharing experiences of God's interaction can be inspirational and can expand one's understanding of God's activity.

## Elizabeth Barberi

Elizabeth Barberi began speaking on prayer and meditation in 1976 and has presented programs in many east coast states. She draws upon insights from the Bible, the practice of Methodist faith healer Olga Worrell, the Edgar Cayce Readings on meditation and prayer, the experiences of some outstanding figures in Christian history, Evelyn Underhill's doctoral study of mysticism, and personal experience. She presents programs on meditation, prayer and dream interpretation for churches, new age gatherings, continuing education programs and other groups.

While raising children Elizabeth explored alternative medicine, started a business, and worked in many community organizations. She was featured in *U.S. News and World Report*, and was awarded certificates by the Berkshire Center for Psychosynthesis, the Association for Research and Enlightenment, and the Commission on Human Relations of Montgomery County MD.

Elizabeth attends services of many religions, but Christianity has always been her home. As a Protestant and as a Catholic (at different times in her life) she has been an active church member. She has practiced meditation forty years. Elizabeth and her husband share life in rural New England.